JAMES RUSSELL LOWELL

POEMS

•

JAMES
RUSSELL
LOWELL

WILDSIDE PRESS

TABLE OF CONTENTS.

iv   Contents.

Contents.

POEMS.

APPLEDORE.

How looks Appledore in a storm?
  I have seen it when its crags seemed **frantic,**
  Butting against the maddened Atlantic,
When surge after surge would heap enorme
  Cliffs of Emerald topped with snow,
  That lifted and lifted and then let go
A great white avalanche of thunder,
  A grinding, blinding, deafening ire
Monadnock might have trembled under;
    And the island, whose rock-roots pierce
      below
To where they are warmed with the central
    fire,
You could feel its granite fibres racked,
    As it seemed to plunge with a shudder and
      thrill
    Right at the breast of the swooping hill,
And to rise again, snorting a cataract
Of rage-froth from every cranny and ledge,
    While the sea drew its breath in hoarse and
      deep,

And the next vast breaker curled its edge,
  Gathering itself for a mighty leap.

North, east, and south there are reefs and
        breakers,
    You would never dream of in smooth
        weather,
That toss and gore the sea for acres,
    Bellowing and gnashing and snarling to-
        gether;
Look northward, where Duck Island lies,
And over its crown you will see arise,
Against a background of slaty skies,
    A row of pillars still and white
    That glimmer and then are out of sight,
As if the moon should suddenly kiss,
    While you crossed the gusty desert by night,
The long colonnades of Persepolis,
And then as sudden a darkness should follow
To gulp the whole scene at a single swallow,
The city's ghost, the drear, brown waste,
And the string of camels, clumsy-paced:—
Look southward for White Island light,
    The lantern stands ninety feet o'er the
        tide;
There is first a half-mile of tumult and fight,
Of dash and roar and tumble and fright,
    And surging bewilderment wild and wide,
Where the breakers struggle left and right,
    Then a mile or more of rushing sea,
And then the light-house slim and lone;
And whenever the whole weight of ocean is
        thrown

Full and fair on White Island head,
  A great mist-jotun you will see
  Lifting himself up silently
High and huge o'er the light-house top,
With hands of wavering spray outspread,
  Groping after the little tower,
  That seems to shrink, and shorten and
      cower,
Till the monster's arms of a sudden drop,
  And silently and fruitlessly
  He sinks again into the sea.

You, meanwhile, where drenched you stand,
  Awaken once more to the rush and roar
And on the rock-point tighten your hand,
As you turn and see a valley deep,
  That was not there a moment before,
Suck rattling down between you and a heap
  Of toppling billow, whose instant fall
  Must sink the whole island once for all—
Or watch the silenter, stealthier seas
  Feeling their way to you more and more;
If they once should clutch you high as the
      knees
They would whirl you down like a sprig of
      kelp,
Beyond all reach of hope or help;—
  And such in a storm is Appledore.

TO THE DANDELION.

DEAR common flower, that grow'st beside the
     way,
Fringing the dusty road with harmless gold,
    First pledge of blithesome May,
Which children pluck, and, full of pride, up-
     hold,
High-hearted buccaneers, o'erjoyed that they
An Eldorado in the grass have found,
    Which not the rich earth's amble round
May match in wealth—thou art more dear to
     me
Than all the prouder Summer-blooms may be.

Gold such as thine ne'er drew the Spanish prow
Through the primeval hush of Indian seas,
    Nor wrinkled the lean brow
Of age, to rob the lover's heart of ease;
'Tis the Spring's largess, which she scatters
     now
To rich and poor alike, with lavish hand,
    Though most hearts never understand
To take it at God's value, but pass by
The offered wealth with unrewarded eye.

Thou art my tropics and mine Italy;
To look at thee unlocks a warmer clime;
    The eyes thou givest me

Are in the heart and heed not space or time:
Not in mid June the golden-cuirassed bee
Feels a more Summer-like, warm ravishment
    In the white lily's breezy tent,
His fragrant Sybaris, than I, when first
From the dark green thy yellow circles burst.

Then think I of deep shadows in the grass,
Of meadows where in sun the cattle graze,
    Where, as the breezes pass,
The gleaming rushes lean a thousand ways,
Of leaves that slumber in a cloudy mass,
Or whiten in the wind, of waters blue
    That from the distance sparkle through
Some woodland gap, and of a sky above
Where one white cloud like a stray lamb doth
        move.

My childhood's earliest thoughts are linked
        with thee;
The sight of thee calls back the robin's song,
    Who from the dark old tree
Beside the door, sang clearly all day long,
And I, secure in childish piety,
Listened as if I heard an angel sing
    With news from Heaven, which he did bring
Fresh every day to my untainted ears,
When birds and flowers and I were happy
        peers.

Thou art the type of those meek charities
Which make up half the nobleness of life,
    Those cheap delights the wise

Pluck from the dusty wayside of earth's strife;
Words of frank cheer, glances of friendly eyes,
Love's smallest coin, which yet to some may
        give
    The morsel that may keep alive
A starving heart, and teach it to behold
Some glimpse of God where all before was cold.

Thy winged seeds, whereof the winds take care,
Are like the words of poet and of sage
    Which through the free heaven fare,
And, now unheeded, in another age
Take root, and to the gladdened future bear
That witness which the present would not
        heed,
    Bringing forth many a thought and deed,
And, planted safely in the eternal sky,
Bloom into stars which earth is guided by.

Full of deep love thou art, yet not more full
Than all thy common brethren of the ground,
    Wherein, were we not dull,
Some words of highest wisdom might be found;
Yet earnest faith from day to day may cull
Some syllables, which, rightly joined, can make
    A spell to soothe life's bitterest ache,
And ope Heaven's portals, which are near us
        still,
Yea, nearer ever than the gates of Ill.

How like a prodigal doth nature seem,
When thou, for all thy gold, so common art!
    Thou teachest me to deem

More sacredly of every human heart,
Since each reflects in joy its scanty gleam
Of Heaven, and could some wondrous secret
    show,
   Did we but pay the love we owe,
And with a child's undoubting wisdom look
On all these living pages of God's book.

But let me read thy lesson right or no,
Of one good gift from thee my heart is sure;
   Old I shall never grow
While thou each year dost come to keep me pure
With legends of my childhood; ah, we owe
Well more than half life's holiness to these
   Nature's first lowly influences,
At thought of which the heart's glad doors
    burst ope,
In dreariest days, to welcome peace and hope.

DARA.

When Persia's sceptre trembled in a hand
Wilted by harem-heats, and all the land
   Was hovered over by those vulture ills
That snuff decaying empire from afar,
Then, with a nature balanced as a star,
   Dara arose, a shepherd of the hills.

He, who had governed fleecy subjects well,
Made his own village, by the self-same spell,
   Secure and peaceful as a guarded fold,

Till, gathering strength by slow and wise
      degrees,
Under his sway, to neighbor villages
    Order returned, and faith and justice old.

Now, when it fortuned that a king more wise
Endued the realm with brain and hands and
      eyes,
    He sought on every side men brave and just,
And having heard the mountain-shepherd's
      praise,
How he rendered the mould of elder days,
    To Dara gave a satrapy in trust.

So Dara shepherded a province wide,
Nor in his viceroy's sceptre took more pride
    Than in his crook before ; but Envy finds
More soil in cities than on mountains bare,
And the frank sun of spirits clear and rare
    Breeds poisonous fogs in low and marish
      minds.

Soon it was whispered at the royal ear
That, though wise Dara's province year by year,
    Like a great sponge, drew wealth and plenty
      up,
Yet when he squeezed it at the king's behest,
Some golden drops, more rich than all the rest,
    Went to the filling of his private cup.

For proof, they said that wheresoe'er he went
A chest, beneath whose weight the camel bent,
    Went guarded, and no other eye had seen

What was therein, save only Dara's own,
Yet, when 'twas opened, all his tent was known
  To glow and lighten with heapt jewels' sheen.

The king set forth for Dara's province straight,
Where, as was fit, outside his city's gate
  That viceroy met him with a stately train;
And there, with archers circled, close at hand,
A camel with the chest was seen to stand;
  The king grew red, for thus the guilt was
    plain.

" Open me now," he cried, " yon treasure-
    chest ! "
'Twas done, and only a worn shepherd's vest
  Was found within; some blushed and hung
    the head,
Not Dara; open as the sky's blue roof
He stood, and " O, my lord, behold the proof
  That I was worthy of my trust ! " he said.

For ruling men, lo ! all the charm I had ;
My soul, in those coarse vestments ever clad,
  Still to the unstained past kept true and leal,
Still on these plains could breathe her mount-
    ain air,
And Fortune's heaviest gifts serenely bear,
  Which bend men from the truth, and make
    them reel.

" To govern wisely I had shown small skill
Were I not lord of simple Dara still ;
  That sceptre kept, I cannot lose my way ! "

Strange dew in royal eyes grew round and
    bright
And thrilled the trembling lids; before 'twas
    night
  Two added provinces blessed Dara's sway.

TO J. F. H.

NINE years have slipped like-hour-glass sand
  From life's fast-emptying globe away,
Since last, dear friend, I clasped your hand,
And lingered on the impoverished land,
  Watching the steamer down the bay.

I held the keepsake which you gave,
  Until the dim smoke-pennon curled
O'er the vague rim 'tween sky and wave,
And closed the distance like a grave,
  Leaving me to the outer world;

The old worn world of hurry and heat,
  The young, fresh world of thought and scope;
While you, where silent surges fleet
Tow'rd far sky beaches still and swept,
  Sunk wavering down the ocean-slope.

Come back our ancient walks to tread,
  Old haunts of lost or scattered friends,
Amid the Muses' factories red,
Where song, and smoke, and laughter sped
  The nights to proctor-hunted ends.

Our old familiars are not laid,
  Though snapped our wands and sunk our
    books,
They beckon, not to be gainsaid,
Where, round broad meads which mowers
    wade,
  Smooth Charles his steel-blue sickle crooks;

Where, as the cloudbergs eastward blow,
  From glow to gloom the hillside shifts
Its lakes of rye that surge and flow,
Its plumps of orchard-trees arow,
  Its snowy white-weeds summer drifts.

Or let us to Nantasket, there
  To wander idly as we list,
Whether, on rocky hillocks bare,
Sharp cedar-points, like breakers, tear
  The trailing fringes of gray mist.

Or whether, under skies clear-blown,
  The heightening surfs with foamy din,
Their breeze-caught forelocks backward blown
Against old Neptune's yellow zone,
  Curl slow, and plunge forever in.

For years thrice three, wise Horace said,
  A poem rare let silence bind;
And love may ripen in the shade,
Like ours, for nine long seasons laid
  In crypts and arches of the mind.

That right Falernian friendship old
  Will we, to grace our feast, call up,
And freely pour the juice of gold,
That keeps life's pulses warm and bold,
  Till Death shall break the empty cup.

PROMETHEUS.

ONE after one the stars have risen and set,
Sparkling upon the hoarfrost on my chain:
The Bear that prowled all night about the fold
Of the North-Star, hath shrunk into his den,
Scared by the blithesome footsteps of the
    Dawn,
Whose blushing smile floods all the Orient;
And now bright Lucifer grows less and less,
Into the heaven's blue quiet deep withdrawn.
Sunless and starless all, the desert sky
Arches above me, empty as this heart
For ages hath been empty of all joy
Except to brood upon its silent hope,
As o'er its hope of day the sky doth now.
All night have I heard voices: deeper yet
The deep, low breathing of the silence grew,
While all about, muffled in awe, there stood
Shadows, or forms, or both, clear-felt at heart,
But, when I turned to front them, far along
Only a shudder through the midnight ran,
And the dense stillness wailed me closer round,
But still I heard them wander up and down
That solitude, and flappings of dusk wings

Did mingle with them, whether of those hags
Let slip upon me once from Hades deep,
Or of yet direr torments, if such be,
I could but guess; and then toward me came
A shape as of a woman: very pale
It was, and calm; its cold eyes did not move,
And mine moved not, but only stared on them.
Their moveless awe went through my brain
      like ice;
A skeleton hand seemed clutching at my heart,
And a sharp chill, as if a dank night fog
Suddenly closed me in, was all I felt:
And then, methought, I heard a freezing sigh,
A long, deep, shivering sigh, as from blue lips
Stiffening in death, close to mine ear.   I
      thought
Some doom was close upon me, and I looked
And saw the red moon through the heavy mist,
Just setting, and it seemed as it were falling,
Or reeling to its fall, so dim and dead
And palsy-struck it looked.   Then all sounds
      merged
Into the rising surges of the pines,
Which, leagues below me, clothing the gaunt
      loins
Of ancient Caucasus with hairy strength,
Sent up a murmur in the morning-wind,
Sad as the wail that from the populous earth
All day and night to high Olympus soars,
Fit incense to thy wicked throne, O Jove.

Thy hated name is tossed once more in scorn
From off my lips, for I will tell thy doom.

And are these tears? Nay, do not triumph,
     Jove!
They are wrung from me but by the agonies
Of prophecy, like those sparse drops which fall
From clouds in travail of the lightning, when
The great wave of the storm, high-curled and
     black,
Rolls steadily onward to its thunderous break.
Why art thou made a god of, thou poor type
Of anger, and revenge, and cunning force?
True Power was never born of brutish
     Strength,
Nor sweet Truth suckled at the shaggy dugs
Of that old she-wolf. Are thy thunderbolts,
That scare the darkness for a space, so strong
As the prevailing patience of meek Light,
Who, with the invincible tenderness of peace,
Wins it to be a portion of herself?
Why art thou made a god of, thou, who hast
The never-sleeping terror at thy heart,
That birthright of all tyrants, worse to bear
Than this thy ravening bird on which I smile?
Thou swear'st to free me, if I will unfold
What kind of doom it is whose omen flits
Across thy heart, as o'er a troop of doves
The fearful shadow of the kite. What need
To know that truth whose knowledge cannot
     save?
Evil its errand hath, as well as Good;
When thine is finished, thou art known no
     more:
There is a higher purity than thou,
And higher purity is greater strength;

Thy nature is thy doom, at which thy heart
Trembles behind the thick wall of thy might.
Let man but hope, and thou art straightway
    chilled
With thought of that drear silence and deep
    night
Which, like a dream, shall swallow thee and
    thine:
Let man but will, and thou art god no more;
More capable of ruin than the gold
And ivory that image thee on earth.
He who hurled down the monstrous Titan-
    brood
Blinded with lightnings, with rough thunders
    stunned,
Is weaker than a simple human thought.
My slender voice can shake thee, as the breeze,
That seems but apt to stir a maiden's hair,
Sways huge Oceanus from pole to pole:
For I am still Prometheus, and foreknow
In my wise heart the end and doom of all.

Yes, I am still Prometheus, wiser grown
By years of solitude—that holds apart
The past and future, giving the soul room
To search into itself—and long commune
With this eternal silence—more a god
In my long-suffering and strength to meet
With equal front the direst shafts of fate,
Than thou in thy faint-hearted despotism,
Girt with thy baby-toys of force and wrath.
Yes, I am that Prometheus who brought
    down

The light to man which thou in selfish fear
Had'st to thyself usurped—his by sole right,
For Man hath right to all save Tyranny—
And which shall free him yet from thy frail
    throne.
Tyrants are but the spawn of Ignorance,
Begotten by the slaves they trample on,
Who, could they win a glimmer of the light,
And see that Tyranny is always weakness,
Or Fear with its own bosom ill at ease,
Would laugh away in scorn the sand-wove
    chain
Which their own blindness feigned for ada-
    mant.
Wrong ever builds on quicksands, but the
    Right
To the firm centre lays its moveless base.
The tyrant trembles if the air but stirs
The innocent ringlets of a child's free hair,
And crouches, when the thought of some great
    spirit,
With world-wide murmur, like a rising gale,
Over men's hearts, as over standing corn,
Rushes, and bends them to its own strong
    will.
So shall some thought of mine yet circle earth
And puff away thy crumbling altars, Jove.
And, would'st thou know of my supreme re-
    venge,
Poor tyrant, even now dethroned in heart,
Realmless in soul, as tyrants ever are,
Listen! and tell me if this bitter peak,
This never-glutted vulture, and these chains

Shrink not before it ; for it shall befit
A sorrow-taught, unconquered Titan-heart.
Men, when their death is on them, seem **to**
    stand
On a precipitous crag that overhangs
The abyss of doom, and in that depth to see,
As in a glass, the features dim and huge
Of things to come, the shadows, as it seems,
Of what have been.   Death ever fronts **the**
    wise,
Not fearfully, but with clear promises
Of larger life, on whose broad vans upborne,
Their out-look widens, and they see beyond
The horizon of the Present and the Past,
Even to the very source and end of things.
Such am I now : immortal woe hath made
My heart a seer, and my soul a judge
Between the substance and the shadow **of**
    Truth.
The sure supremeness of the Beautiful,
By all the martyrdoms made doubly sure
Of such as I am, this is my revenge,
Which of my wrongs builds a triumphal **arch**
Through which I see a sceptre and a throne.
The pipings of glad shepherds on the hills,
Tending the flocks no more to bleed for thee—
The songs of maidens pressing with white feet
The vintage on thine altars poured no more—
The murmurous bliss of lovers, underneath
Dim grape-vine bowers, whose rosy bunches
    press
Not half so closely their warm cheeks, **un-**
    scared

By thoughts of thy brute lusts—the hive-like
    hum
Of peaceful commonwealths, where sunburnt
    Toil
Reaps for itself the rich earth made its own
By its own labor, lightened with glad hymns
To an omnipotence which thy mad bolts
Would cope with as a spark with the vast sea,
Even the spirit of free love and peace,
Duty's sure recompense through life and
    death—
These are such harvests as all master-spirits
Reap, haply not on earth, but reap no less
Because the sheaves are bound by hands not
    theirs;
These are the bloodless daggers wherewithal
They stab fallen tyrants, this their high re-
    venge:
For their best part of life on earth is when,
Long after death, prisoned and pent no more,
Their thoughts, their wild dreams even, have
    become
Part of the necessary air men breathe;
When, like the moon, herself behind a cloud,
They shed down light before us on life's sea,
That cheers us to steer onward still in hope.
Earth with her twining memories ivies o'er
Their holy sepulchres, the chainless sea
In tempest or wide calm repeats their
    thoughts,
The lightning and the thunder, all free things,
Have legends of them for the ears of men.
All other glories are as falling stars,

But universal Nature watches theirs;
Such strength is won by love of human kind.

Not that I feel that hunger after fame,
Which souls of a half-greatness are beset with;
But that the memory of noble deeds
Cries shame upon the idle and the vile,
And keeps the heart of Man for ever up
To the heroic level of old time.
To be forgot at first is little pain
To a heart conscious of such high intent
As must be deathless on the lips of men;
But, having been a name, to sink and be
A something which the world can do without,
Which, having been or not, would never
     change
The lightest pulse of fate—this is indeed
A cup of bitterness the worst to taste,
And this thy heart shall empty to the dregs.
Oblivion is lonelier than this peak—
Behold thy destiny! Thou think'st it much
That I should brave thee, miserable god!
But I have braved a mightier than thou,
Even the temptings of this soaring heart
Which might have made me, scarcely less
     than thou,
A god among my brethren weak and blind
Scarce less than thou, a pitiable thing,
To be down-trodden into darkness soon.
But now I am above thee, for thou art
The bungling workmanship of fear, the block
That scarce the swart Barbarian; but I
Am what myself have made, a nature wise

With finding in itself the types of all,—
With watching from the dim verge of the
     time
What things to be are visible in the gleams
Thrown forward on them from the luminous
     past—
Wise with the history of its own frail heart,
With reverence and sorrow, and with love
Broad as the world for freedom and for man.

Thou and all strength shall crumble, except
     Love,
By whom and for whose glory ye shall cease:
And, when thou art but a dim moaning heard
From out the pitiless glooms of Chaos, I
Shall be a power and a memory,
A name to scare all tyrants with, a light
Unsetting as the pole-star, a great voice
Heard in the breathless pauses of the fight
By truth and freedom ever waged with wrong,
Clear as a silver trumpet, to awake
Huge echoes that from age to age live on
In kindred spirits, giving them a sense
Of boundless power from boundless suffering
     wrung.
And many a glazing eye shall smile to see
The memory of my triumph (for to meet
Wrong with endurance, and to overcome
The present with a heart that looks beyond,
Are triumph), like a prophet eagle, perch
Upon the sacred banner of the right.
Evil springs up, and flowers, and bears nc
     seed,

And feeds the green earth with its swift
    decay,
Leaving it richer for the growth of truth;
But Good, once put in action or in thought,
Like a strong oak, doth from its boughs shed
    down
The ripe germs of a forest. Thou, weak god,

Shalt fade and be forgotten; but this soul,
Fresh-living still in the serene abyss,
In every heaving shall partake, that grows
From heart to heart among the sons of men—
As the ominous hum before the earthquake
    runs
Far through the Ægean from roused isle to
    isle—
Foreboding wreck to palaces and shrines,
And mighty rents in many a cavernous error
That darkens the free light to man :—This
    heart
Unscarred by the grim vulture, as the truth
Grows but more lovely 'neath the beaks and
    claws
Of Harpies blind that fain would soil it, shall
In all the throbbing exultations share
That wait on freedom's triumphs, and in all
The glorious agonies of martyr-spirits—
Sharp lightning-throes to split the jagged
    clouds
That veil the future, showing them the end—
Pain's thorny crown for constancy and truth,
Girding the temples like a wreath of stars.
This is a thought, that, like the fabled laurel,

Makes my faith thunder-proof, and thy dread
　　bolts
Fall on me like the silent flakes of snow
On the hoar brows of aged Caucasus :
But, O thought far more blissful, they can rend
This cloud of flesh, and make my soul a star !

Unleash thy crouching thunders now, O Jove!
Free this high heart which, a poor captive
　　long,
Doth knock to be let forth, this heart which
　　still,
In its invincible manhood, overtops
Thy puny godship as this mountain doth
The pines that moss its roots.　O even now,
While from my peak of suffering I look down,
Beholding with a far-spread gush of hope
The sunrise of that Beauty in whose face,
Shone all around with love, no man shall look
But straightway like a god he is uplift
Unto the throne long empty for his sake,
And clearly oft foreshadowed in wide dreams
By his free inward nature, which nor thou,
Nor any anarch after thee, can bind
From working its great doom—now, now set
　　free
This essence, not to die, but to become
Part of that awful Presence which doth haunt
The palaces of tyrants, to scare off,
With its grim eyes and fearful whisperings
And hideous sense of utter loneliness,
All hope of safety, all desire of peace,
All but the loathed forefeeling of blank death—

Part of that spirit which doth ever brood
In patient calm on the unpilfered nest
Of man's deep heart, till mighty thoughts grow
    fledged
To sail with darkening shadow o'er the world,
Until they swoop, and their pale quarry make
Of some o'erbloated wrong—that spirit which
Scatters great hopes in the seed-field of man,
Like acorns among grain, to grow and be
A roof for freedom in all coming time.

But no, this cannot be; for ages yet,
In solitude unbroken, shall I hear
The angry Caspian to the Euxine shout,
And Euxine answer with a muffled roar,
On either side storming the giant walls
Of Caucasus with leagues of climbing foam,
(Less, from my height, than flakes of downy
    snow),
That draw back baffled but to hurl again,
Snatched up in wrath and horrible turmoil,
Mountain on mountain, as the Titans erst,
My brethren, scaling the high seat of Jove,
Heaved Pelion upon Ossa's shoulders broad,
In vain emprise. The moon will come and go
With her monotonous vicissitude;
Once beautiful, when I was free to walk
Among my fellows and to interchange
The influence benign of loving eyes,
But now by aged use grown wearisome;—
False thought! most false! for how could I
    endure
These crawling centuries of lonely woe

Unshamed by weak complaining, but for thee,
Loneliest, save me, of all created things,
Mild-eyed Astartè, my best comforter,
With thy pale smile of sad benignity?
Year after year will pass away and seem
To me, in mine eternal agony,
But as the shadows of dumb summer-clouds,
Which I have watched so often darkening o'er
The vast Sarmatian plain, league-wide at first,
But, with still swiftness, lessening on and on
Till cloud and shadow meet and mingle where
The grey horizon fades into the sky,
Far, far to northward. Yes, for ages yet
Must I lie here upon my altar huge,
A sacrifice for man. Sorrow will be,
As it hath been, his portion; endless doom,
While the immortal with the mortal linked
Dreams of its wings and pines for what it
    dreams
With upward yearn unceasing. Better so:
For wisdom is meek sorrow's patient child,
And empire over self, and all the deep
Strong charities that make men seem like
    gods;
And love, that makes them be gods, from her
    breasts
Sucks in the milk that makes mankind one
    blood.
Good never comes unmixed, or so it seems,
Having two faces, as some images
Are carved, of foolish gods; one face is ill,
But one heart lies beneath, and that is good,
As are all hearts, when we explore their depths.

Therefore, great heart, bear up! thou art but
  type
Of what all lofty spirits endure, that fain
Would win men back to strength and peace
  through love:
Each hath his lonely peak, and on each heart
Envy, or scorn, or hatred, tears lifelong
With vulture beak; yet the high soul is left,
And faith, which is but hope grown wise, and
  love,
And patience which at last shall overcome.

  Cambridge, Mass., June, 1843.

ROSALINE.

Thou look'd'st on me all yesternight,
Thine eyes were blue, thy hair was bright
As when we murmured our trothplight
Beneath the thick stars, Rosaline!
Thy hair was braided on thy head
As on the day we two were wed,
Mine eyes scarce knew if thou wert dead—
But my shrunk heart knew, Rosaline!

The deathwatch tickt behind the wall,
The blackness rustled like a pall,
The moaning wind did rise and fall
Among the bleak pines, Rosaline!
My heart beat thickly in mine ears:

The lids may shut out fleshly fears,
But still the spirit sees and hears,
Its eyes are lidless, Rosaline!

A wildness rushing suddenly,
A knowing some ill shape is nigh,
A wish for death, a fear to die—
Is not this vengeance, Rosaline!
A loneliness that is not lone,
A love quite withered up and gone,
A strong soul trampled from its throne—
What would'st thou further, Rosaline!

'Tis lone such moonless nights as these,
Strange sounds are out upon the breeze,
And the leaves shiver in the trees,
And then thou comest, Rosaline!
I seem to hear the mourners go,
With long black garments trailing slow,
And plumes anodding to and fro,
As once I heard them, Rosaline!

Thy shroud it is of snowy white,
And, in the middle of the night,
Thou standest moveless and upright,
Gazing upon me, Rosaline!
There is no sorrow in thine eyes,
But evermore that meek surprise—
Oh, God! her gentle spirit tries
To deem me guiltless, Rosaline!

Above thy grave the Robin sings,
And swarms of bright and happy things

Flit all about with sunlit wings—
But I am cheerless, Rosaline!
The violets on the hillock toss,
The gravestone is o'ergrown with moss,
For nature feels not any loss—
But I am cheerless, Rosaline!

Ah! why wert thou so lowly bred?
Why was my pride galled on to wed
Her who brought lands and gold instead
Of thy heart's treasure, Rosaline!
Why did I fear to let thee stay
To look on me and pass away
Forgivingly, as in its May,
A broken flower, Rosaline!

I thought not, when my dagger strook,
Of thy blue eyes; I could not brook
The past all pleading in one look
Of utter sorrow, Rosaline!
I did not know when thou wert dead:
A blackbird whistling overhead
Thrilled through my brain; I would have fled
But dared not leave thee, Rosaline!

A low, low moan, a light twig stirred
By the upspringing of a bird,
A drip of blood—were all I heard—
Then deathly stillness, Rosaline!
The sun rolled down, and very soon,
Like a great fire, the awful moon
Rose, stained with blood, and then a swoon
Crept chilly o'er me, Rosaline!

The stars came out; and, one by one,
Each angel from his silver throne
Looked down and saw what I had done:
I dared not hide me, Rosaline!
I crouched; I feared thy corpse would cry
Against me to God's quiet sky,
I thought I saw the blue lips try
To utter something, Rosaline!

I waited with a maddened grin
To hear that voice all icy thin
Slide forth and tell my deadly sin
To hell and Heaven, Rosaline!
But no voice came, and then it seemed
That if the very corpse had screamed
The sound like sunshine glad had streamed
Through that dark stillness, Rosaline!

Dreams of old quiet glimmered by,
And faces loved in infancy
Came and looked on me mournfully,
Till my heart melted, Rosaline!
I saw my mother's dying bed,
I heard her bless me, and I shed
Cool tears—but lo! the ghastly dead
Stared me to madness, Rosaline!

And then amid the silent night
I screamed with horrible delight,
And in my brain an awful light
Did seem to crackle, Rosaline!
It is my curse! sweet mem'ries fall
From me like snow—and only all

Of that one night, like cold worms crawl
My doomed heart over, Rosaline!

Thine eyes are shut: they nevermore
Will leap thy gentle words before
To tell the secret o'er and o'er
Thou could'st not smother, Rosaline!
Thine eyes are shut: they will not shine
With happy tears, or, through the vine
That hid thy casement, beam on mine
Sunfull with gladness, Rosaline!

Thy voice I nevermore shall hear,
Which in old times did seem so dear,
That, ere it trembled in mine ear,
My quick heart heard it, Rosaline!
Would I might die!   I were as well,
Ay, better, at my home in Hell,
To set for aye a burning spell
'Twixt me and memory, Rosaline!

Why wilt thou haunt me with thine eyes,
Wherein such blessed memories,
Such pitying forgiveness lies,   ·
Than hate more bitter, Rosaline!
Woe 's me! I know that love so high
As thine, true soul, could never die,
And with mean clay in church-yard lie—
Would God it were so, Rosaline!

3

SONNET.

If some small savor creep into my rhyme
Of the old poets, if some words I use,
Neglected long, which have the lusty thews
Of that gold-haired and earnest-hearted time,
Whose loving joy and sorrow all sublime
Have given our tongue its starry eminence,—
It is not pride, God knows, but reverence
Which hath grown in me since my childhood's
     prime ;
Wherein I feel that my poor lyre is strung
With soul-strings like to theirs, and that I have
No right to muse their holy graves among,
If I can be a custom-fettered slave,
And, in mine own true spirit, am not brave
To speak what rusheth upward to my tongue.

A GLANCE BEHIND THE CURTAIN.

We see but half the causes of our deeds,
Seeking them wholly in the outer life,
And heedless of the encircling spirit-world
Which, though unseen, is felt, and sows in us
All germs of pure and world-wide purposes.
From one stage of our being to the next
We pass unconscious o'er a slender bridge,

The momentary work of unseen hands,
Which crumbles down behind us; looking
    back,
We see the other shore, the gulf between,
And, marvelling how we won to where we
    stand,
Content ourselves to call the builder Chance.
We trace the wisdom to the apple's fall,
Not to the soul of Newton, ripe with all
The hoarded thoughtfulness of earnest years,
And waiting but one ray of sunlight more
To blossom fully.

                  But whence came that ray?
We call our sorrows destiny, but ought
Rather to name our high successes so.
Only the instincts of great souls are Fate,
And have predestined sway: all other things,
Except by leave of us, could never be.
For Destiny is but the breath of God
Still moving in us, the last fragment left
Of our unfallen nature, waking oft
Within our thought to beckon us beyond
The narrow circle of the seen and known,
And always tending to a noble end,
As all things must that overrule the soul,
And for a space unseat the helmsman, Will.
The fate of England and of freedom once
Seemed wavering in the heart of one plain
    man:
One step of his, and the great dial-hand
That marks the destined progress of the world
In the eternal round from wisdom on

To higher wisdom, had been made to pause
A hundred years.   That step he did not take—
He knew not why, nor we, but only God—
And lived to make his simple oaken chair
More terrible and grandly beautiful,
More full of majesty, than any throne,
Before or after, of a British king.

Upon the pier stood two stern-visaged men,
Looking to where a little craft lay moored,
Swayed by the lazy current of the Thames,
Which weltered by in muddy listlessness.
Grave men they were, and battlings of fierce
     thought
Had scared away all softness from their brows,
And ploughed rough furrows there before their
     time.
Care, not of self, but of the common weal,
Had robbed their eyes of youth, and left in-
     stead
A look of patient power and iron will,
And something fiercer, too, that gave broad
     hint
Of the plain weapons girded at their sides.
The younger had an aspect of command—
Not such as trickles down, a slender stream,
In the shrunk channel of a great descent—
But such as lies entowered in heart and head,
And an arm prompt to do the 'hests of both.
His was a brow where gold were out of place,
And yet it seemed right worthy of a crown
(Though he despised such), were it only made
Of iron, or some serviceable stuff

That would have matched his sinewy brown
    face.
The elder, although such he hardly seemed
(Care makes so little of some five short years),
Bore a clear, honest face, where scholarship
Had mildened somewhat of its rougher strength,
To sober courage, such as best befits
The unsullied temper of a well-taught mind,
Yet left it so as one could plainly guess
The pent volcano smouldering underneath.
He spoke: the other, hearing, kept his gaze
Still fixed, as on some problem in the sky.

" O, CROMWELL, we are fallen on evil times!
There was a day when England had wide
    room
For honest men as well as foolish kings ;
But now the uneasy stomach of the time
Turns squeamish at them both.   Therefore let
    us
Seek out that savage clime where men as yet
Are free: there sleeps the vessel on the tide,
Her languid sails but drooping for the wind :
All things are fitly cared for, and the Lord
Will watch as kindly o'er the Exodus
Of us His servants now, as in old time.
We have no cloud or fire, and haply we
May not pass dryshod through the ocean-
    stream ;
But, saved or lost, all things are in His hand."
So spake he, and meantime the other stood
With wide, grey eyes still reading the blank
    air,

As if upon the sky's blue wall he saw
Some mystic sentence written by a hand
Such as of old did scare the Assyrian king,
Girt with his satraps in the blazing feast.

" HAMPDEN, a moment since, my purpose was
To fly with thee—for I will call it flight,
Nor flatter it with any smoother name—
But something in me bids me not to go;
And I am one, thou knowest, who, unscared
By what the weak deem omens, yet give heed
And reverence due to whatsoe'er my soul
Whispers of warning to the inner ear.
Why should we fly? Nay, why not rather
        stay
And rear again our Zion's crumbled walls,
Not as of old the walls of Thebes were built
By minstrel twanging, but, if need should be,
With the more potent music of our swords?
Think'st thou that score of men beyond the sea
Claim more God's care than all of England
        here?
No: when He moves His arm, it is to aid
Whole peoples, heedless if a few be crushed,
As some are ever when the destiny
Of man takes one stride onward nearer home.
Believe it, 'tis the mass of men He loves,
And where there is most sorrow and most
        want,
Where the high heart of man is trodden down
The most, 'tis not because He hides His face
From them in wrath, as purblind teachers
        prate.

Not so : there most is He, for there is He
Most needed.　Men who seek for Fate abroad
Are not so near His heart as they who dare
Frankly to face her where she faces them,
On their own threshold, where their souls are
　　　strong
To grapple with and throw her, as I once,
Being yet a boy, did throw this puny king,
Who now has grown so dotard as to deem
That he can wrestle with an angry realm,
And throw the brawned Antæus of men's rights.
No, Hampden ; they have half-way conquered
　　　Fate
Who go half-way to meet her—as will I.
Freedom hath yet a work for me to do ;
So speaks that inward voice which never yet
Spake falsely, when it urged the spirit on
To noble deeds for country and mankind.

" What should we do in that small colony
Of pinched fanatics, who would rather choose
Freedom to clip an inch more from their hair
Than the great chance of setting England free ?
Not there amid the stormy wilderness
Should we learn wisdom ; or, if learned, what
　　　room
To put it into act—else worse than naught?
We learn our souls more, tossing for an hour
Upon this huge and ever vexed sea
Of human thought, where kingdoms go to wreck
Like fragile bubbles yonder in the stream,
Than in a cycle of New England sloth,
Broke only by some petty Indian war,

Or quarrel for a letter, more or less,
In some hard word, which, spelt in either way,
Not their most learned clerks can understand.
New times demand new measures and new
    men;
The world advances, and in time outgrows
The laws that in our father's day were best ;
And, doubltess, after us, some purer scheme
Will be shaped out by wiser men than we,
Made wiser by the steady growth of truth.
We cannot bring Utopia at once ;
But better almost be at work in sin
Than in a brute inaction browse and sleep.
No man is born into the world whose work
Is not born with him; there is always work,
And tools to work withal, for those who will ;
And blessed are the horny hands of toil !
The busy world shoves angrily aside
The man who stands with arms akimbo set,
Until occasion tells him what to do;
And he who waits to have his task marked
    out,
Shall die and leave his errand unfulfilled.
Our time is one that calls for earnest deeds.
Reason and Government, like two broad
    seas,
Yearn for each other with outstretched arms
Across this narrow isthmus of the throne,
And roll their white surf higher every day.
The field lies wide before us, where to reap
The easy harvest of a deathless name,
Though with no beter sickles than our swords.
My soul is not a palace of the past,

Where outworn creeds, like Rome's grey senate,
    quake,
Hearing afar the Vandal's trumpet hoarse,
That shakes old systems with a thunder-fit.
The time is ripe, and rotten-ripe, for change;
Then let it come : I have no dread of what
Is called for, by the instinct of mankind.
Nor think I that God's world would fall apart
Because we tear a parchment more or less.
Truth is eternal, but her effluence,
With endless change, is fitted to the hour;
Her mirror is turned forward, to reflect
The promise of the future, not the past.
I do not fear to follow out the truth,
Albeit along the precipice's edge.
Let us speak plain : there is more force in
    names
Than most men dream of ; and a lie may keep
Its throne a whole age longer, if it skulk
Behind the shield of some fair-seeming name.
Let us call tyrants *tyrants*, and maintain
That only freedom comes by grace of God,
And all that comes not by His grace must fall;
For men in earnest have no time to waste
In patching fig-leaves for the naked truth.

" I will have one more grapple with the man
Charles Stuart : whom the boy o'ercame,
The man stands not in awe of.   I perchance
Am one raised up by the Almighty arm
To witness some great truth to all the world.
Souls destined to o'erleap the vulgar lot,
And mould the world unto the scheme of God,

Have a foreconsciousness of their high doom,
As men are known to shiver at the heart,
When the cold shadow of some coming ill
Creeps slowly o'er their spirits unawares ·
Hath Good less power of prophecy than Ill?
How else could men whom God hath called to
    sway
Earth's rudder, and to steer the barque of
    Truth,
Beating against the wind toward her port,
Bear all the mean and buzzing grievances,
The petty martydroms wherewith Sin strives
To weary out the tethered hope of Faith,
The sneers, the unrecognizing look of friends,
Who worship the dead corpse of old king
    Custom,
Where it doth lie in state within the Church,
Striving to cover up the mighty ocean
With a man's palm, and making even the truth
Lie for them, holding up the glass reversed,
To make the hope of man seem further off?
My God! when I read o'er the bitter lives
Of men whose eager hearts were quite too
    great
To beat beneath the cramped mode of the day,
And see them mocked at by the world they love,
Haggling with prejudice for pennyworths
Of that reform which their hard toil will make
The common birthright of the age to come—
When I see this, spite of my faith in God,
I marvel how their hearts bear up so long;
Nor could they, but for this same prophecy,
This inward feeling of the glorious end.

" Deem me not fond ; but in my warmer youth,
Ere my heart's bloom was soiled and brushed
    away,
I had great dreams of mighty things to come ;
Of conquest ; whether by the sword or pen,
I knew not ; but some conquest I would have,
Or else swift death : now, wiser grown in
    years,
I find youth's dreams are but the flutterings
Of those strong wings whereon the soul shall
    soar
In after time to win a starry throne ;
And therefore cherish them, for they were lots
Which I, a boy, cast in the helm of Fate.
Nor will I draw them, since a man's right hand,
A right hand guided by an earnest soul,
With a true instinct, takes the golden prize
From out a thousand blanks.   What men call
    luck,
Is the prerogative of valiant souls,
The feality life pays its rightful kings.
The helm is shaking now, and I will stay
To pluck my lot forth ; it were sin to flee ! "

So they two turned together ; one to die
Fighting for freedom on the bloody field ;
The other, far more happy, to become
A name earth wears for ever next her heart ;
One of the few that have a right to rank
With the true Makers ; for his spirit wrought
Order from Chaos ; proved that right divine
Dwelt only in the excellence of Truth ;
And far within old Darkness' hostile lines

Advanced and pitched the shining tents of
    Light.
Nor shall the grateful Muse forget to tell,
That—not the least among his many claims
To deathless honor—he was MILTON's friend,
A man not second among those who lived
To show us that the poet's lyre demands
An arm of tougher sinew than the sword.

A SONG.

Violet! sweet violet!
Thine eyes are full of tears;
    Are they wet
    Even yet
With the thought of other years,
Or with gladness are they full,
For the night so beautiful,
And longing for those far-off spheres?

Loved one of my youth thou wast,
Of my merry youth,
    And I see,
    Tearfully,
    All the fair and sunny past,
All its openness and truth,
Ever fresh and green in thee
As the moss is in the sea.

Thy little heart, that hath with love
Grown colored like the sky above,

On which thou lookest ever,—
    Can it know
    All the woe
Of hope for what returneth never,
All the sorrow and the longing
To these hearts of ours belonging!

    Out on it! no foolish pining
        For the sky
        Dims thine eye,
Or for the stars so calmly shining;
Like thee let this soul of mine
Take hue from that wherefor I long,
Self-stayed and high, serene and strong
Not satisfied with hoping—but divine.

    Violet! dear violet!
    Thy blue eyes are only wet
With joy and love of him who sent thee,
And for the fulfilling sense
Of that glad obedience
Which made thee all which Nature meant thee!

THE MOON.

    My soul was like the sea
        Before the moon was made;
    Moaning in vague immensity,
        Of its own strength afraid,
        Unrestful and unstaid.
    Through every rift it foamed in vain
        About its earthly prison,

Seeking some unknown thing in pain
And sinking restless back again,

   For yet no moon had risen :
Its only voice a vast dumb moan
Of utterless anguish speaking,
It lay unhopefully alone
And lived but in an aimless seeking.

So was my soul : but when 't was full
   Of unrest to o'erloading,
A voice of something beautiful
   Whispered a dim foreboding,
And yet so soft, so sweet, so low,
It had not more of joy than woe:
And, as the sea doth oft lie still,
   Making his waters meet,
As if by an unconscious will,
   For the moon's silver feet,
Like some serene, unwinking eye
That waits a certain destiny,
So lay my soul within mine eyes
When thou its sovereign moon didst rise.

And now, howe'er its waves above
   May toss and seem uneaseful,
One strong, eternal law of love
   With guidance sure and peaceful,
As calm and natural as breath
Moves its great deeps through Life and Death.

THE FATHERLAND.

Where is the true man's fatherland?
  Is it where he by chance is born?
  Doth not the free-winged spirit scorn
In such pent borders to be spanned?
  Oh yes, his fatherland must be
  As the blue heavens wide and free!

Is it alone where freedom is,
  Where God is God and man is man?
  Doth he not claim a broader span
For the soul's love of home than this?
  Oh yes! his fatherland must be
  As the blue heavens wide and free!

Where'er a human heart doth wear
  Joy's myrtle wreath, or sorrow's gyves,
  Where'er a human spirit strives
After a life more pure and fair,
  There is the true man's birthplace grand!
  His is a world-wide fatherland!

Where'er a single slave doth pine,
  Where'er one man may help another—
  Thank God for such a birthright, brother!
That spot of earth is thine and mine;
  There is the true man's birthplace grand!
  His is a world-wide fatherland!

A PARABLE.

Worn and footsore was the Prophet
　When he reached the holy hill;
"God has left the earth," he murmured,
　" Here his presence lingers still.

"God of all the olden prophets,
　Wilt thou talk with me no more?
Have I not as truly loved thee
　As thy chosen ones of yore?

" Hear me, guider of my fathers,
　Lo, an humble heart is mine;
By thy mercy I beseech thee,
　Grant thy servant but a sign!"

Bowing then his head, he listened
　For an answer to his prayer;
No loud burst of thunder followed,
　Not a murmur stirred the air:

But the tuft of moss before him
　Opened while he waited yet,
And from out the rock's hard bosom
　Sprang a tender violet.

"God! I thank thee," said the Prophet,
　" Hard of heart and blind was I,

Looking to the holy mountain
  For the gift of prophecy.

"Still thou speakest with thy children
  Freely as in Eld sublime,
Humbleness and love and patience
  Give dominion over Time.

" Had I trusted in my nature,
  And had faith in lowly things,
Thou thyself wouldst then have sought me,
  And set free my spirit's wings.

" But I looked for signs and wonders
  That o'er men should give me sway;
Thirsting to be more than mortal,
  I was even less than clay.

" Ere I entered on my journey,
  As I girt my loins to start,
Ran to me my little daughter,
  The beloved of my heart;

" In her hand she held a flower,
  Like to this as like may be,
Which beside my very threshold
  She had plucked and brought to me."
  4

ON THE DEATH OF A FRIEND'S CHILD.

DEATH never came so nigh to me before,
Nor showed me his mild face: Oft I had
    mused
Of calm and peace and deep forgetfulness,
Of folded hands, closed eyes, and heart at
    rest,
And slumber sound beneath a flowery turf,
Of faults forgotten, and an inner place
Kept sacred for us in the heart of friends;
But these were idle fancies satisfied
With the mere husk of this great Mystery,
And dwelling in the outward shows of things.
Heaven is not mounted to on wings of dreams,
Nor doth the unthankful happiness of youth
Aim thitherward, but floats from bloom to
    bloom,
With earth's warm patch of sunshine well
    content:
'Tis sorrow builds the shining ladder up
Whose golden rounds are our calamities,
Whereon our firm feet planting, nearer God
The spirit climbs, and hath its eyes unsealed.

True is it that Death's face seems stern and
    cold,
When he is sent to summon those we love,
But all God's angels come to us disguised;

Sorrow and sickness, poverty and death,
One after other lift their frowning masks,
And we behold the seraph's face beneath,
All radiant with the glory and the calm
Of having looked upon the smile of God.
With every anguish of our earthly past
The spirit's sight grows clearer; this was
      meant
When Jesus touched the blind man's lids with
      clay.
Life is the jailor, Death the angel sent
To draw the unwilling bolts and set us free.
He flings not ope the ivory gate of Rest—
Only the fallen spirit knocks at that—
But to benigner regions beckons us,
To destinies of more rewarded toil.

In the hushed chamber, sitting by the dead,
It grates on us to hear the flood of life
Whirl rustling onward, senseless of our loss.
The bee hums on; around the blossomed vine
Whirrs the light humming-bird; the cricket
      chirps;
The locust's shrill alarum stings the ear;
Hard by, the cock shouts lustily; from farm
      to farm,
His cheery brothers, telling of the sun,
Answer, till far away the joyance dies;
We never knew before how God had filled
The summer air with happy living sounds;
All round us seems an overplus of life,
And yet the one dear heart lies cold and still.
It is most strange, when the great Miracle

Hath for our sakes been done; when we have
    had
Our inwardest experience of God,
When with his presence still the room ex-
    pands,
And is awed after him, that naught is changed,
That Nature's face looks unacknowledging,
And the mad world still dances heedless on
After its butterflies, and gives no sigh.
'Tis hard at first to see it all aright;
In vain Faith blows her trump to summon back
Her scattered troop; yet, through the clouded
    glass
Of our own bitter tears, we learn to look
Undazzled on the kindness of God's face;
Earth is too dark, and Heaven alone shines
    through.

How changed, dear friend, are thy part and thy
    child's!
He bends above *thy* cradle now, or holds
His warning finger out to be thy guide;
Thou art the nursling now; he watches thee
Slow learning, one by one, the secret things
Which are to him used sights of every day;
He smiles to see thy wondering glances con
The grass and pebbles of the spirit world,
To thee miraculous; and he will teach
Thy knees their due observances of prayer.

Children are God's apostles, day by day,
Sent forth to preach of love, and hope, and
    peace;

Nor hath thy babe his mission left undone.
To me, at least, his going hence hath given
Serener thoughts and nearer to the skies,
And opened a new fountain in my heart
For thee, my friend, and all: and oh, if Death
More near approaches, meditates, and clasps
Even now some dearer, more reluctant hand,
God, strengthen thou my faith, that I may see
That 'tis thine angel who, with loving haste,
Unto the service of the inner shrine
Doth waken thy beloved with a kiss!

   Cambridge, Mass., Sept 3d, 1844.

AN INCIDENT IN A RAILROAD CAR.

HE spoke ot Burns; men rude and rough
   Pressed round to hear the praise of one
Whose breast was made of manly, simple stuff,
   As homespun as their own.

And, when he read, they forward leaned
   And heard, with eager hearts and ears,
His birdlike songs whom glory never weaned
   From humble smiles and tears.

Slowly there grew a tender awe,
   Sunlike o'er faces brown and hard,
As if in him who read they felt and saw
   Some presence of the bard.

It was a sight for sin and wrong,
   And slavish tyranny to see,

A sight to make our faith more pure and strong
  In high Humanity.

1 thought, these men will carry hence,
  Promptings their former life above,
And something of a finer reverence
  For beauty, truth, and love.

God scatters love on every side,
  Freely among his children all,
And always hearts are lying open wide
  Wherein some grains may fall.

There is no wind but sows some seeds
  Of a more true and open life,
Which burst unlooked for into high-souled
    deeds
  With wayside beauty rife.

We find within these souls of ours
  Some wild germs of a higher birth,
Which in the poet's tropic heart bears flowers
  Whose fragrance fills the earth.

Within the hearts of all men lie
  These promises of wider bliss,
Which blossom into hopes that cannot die,
  In sunny hours like this.

All that hath been majestical
  In life or death since time began,
Is native in the simple heart of all,
  The angel heart of man.

And thus among the untaught poor
  Great deeds and feelings find a home
Which casts in shadow all the golden lore
  Of classic Greece or Rome.

Oh! mighty brother-soul of man,
  Where'er thou art, in low or high,
Thy skyey arches with exulting span
  O'er-roof infinity.

All thoughts that mould the age begin
  Deep down within the primitive soul,
And, from the many, slowly upward wing
  To One who grasps the whole.

In his broad breast, the feeling deep
  Which struggled on the many's tongue,
Swells to a tide of Thought whose surges
    leap
  O'er the weak throne of wrong.

Never did poesy appear
  So full of Heav'n to me as when
I saw how it would pierce through pride and
    fear,
  To lives of coarsest men.

It may be glorious to write
  Thoughts that shall glad the two or three
High souls like those far stars that come in
    sight
  Once in a century.

But better far it is to speak
　One simple word which now and then
Shall waken their free nature in the weak
　And friendless sons of men ;

To write some earnest verse or line
　Which, seeking not the praise of Art,
Shall make a clearer faith and manhood shine
　In the unlearned heart.
　　　Boston, April, 1842.

AN INCIDENT OF THE FIRE AT
HAMBURGH.

THE tower of old Saint Nicholas soared upward
　to the skies,
Like some huge piece of nature's make, the
　growth of centuries ;
You could not deem its crowding spires a work
　of human art,
They seemed to struggle lightward so from a
　sturdy living heart.

Not Nature's self more freely speaks in crystal
　or in oak
Than, through the pious builder's hand, in that
　gray pile she spoke ;
And as from acorn springs the oak, so, freely
　and alone,
Sprang from his heart this hymn to God, sung
　in obedient stone.

It seemed a wondrous freak of chance, so
  perfect, yet so rough,
A whim of Nature crystallized slowly in
  granite tough;
The thick spires yearned toward the sky in
  quaint harmonious lines,
And in broad sunlight basked and slept, like a
  grove of blasted pines.

Never did rock or stream or tree lay claim with
  better right
To all the adorning sympathies of shadow and
  of light;
And, in that forest petrified, as forester there
  dwells
Stout Herman, the old sacristan, sole lord of
  all its bells.

Surge leaping after surge, the fire roared
  onward, red as blood,
Till half of Hamburgh lay engulfed beneath the
  eddying flood;
For miles away, the fiery spray poured down
  its deadly rain,
And back and forth the billows drew, and
  paused, and broke again.

From square to square, with tiger leaps, still
  on and on it came;
The air to leeward trembled with the pantings
  of the flame,

And church and palace, which even now stood
    whelmed but to the knee,
Lift their black roofs like breakers lone amid
    the rushing sea.

Up in his tower old Herman sat and watched
    with quiet look;
His soul had trusted God too long to be at last
    forsook:
He could not fear, for surely God a pathway
    would unfold
Through this red sea, for faithful hearts, as
    once he did of old.

But scarcely can he cross himself, or on his
    good saint call,
Before the sacrilegious flood o'erleaped the
    churchyard wall,
And, ere a *pater* half was said, 'mid smoke and
    crackling glare,
His island tower scarce juts its head above the
    wide despair.

Upon the peril's desperate peak his heart stood
    up sublime;
His first thought was for God above, his next
    was for his chime;
"Sing now, and make your voices heard in
    hymns of praise," cried he,
"As did the Israelites of old, safe-walking
    through the sea!

"Through this red sea our God hath made
    our pathway safe to shore;
 Our promised land stands full in sight; shout
    now as ne'er before."
And, as the tower came crashing down, the
    bells, in clear accord,
Pealed forth the grand old German hymn—
    "All good souls praise the Lord!"

SONNETS.

I.

As the broad ocean endlessly upheaveth,
  With the majestic beating of his heart,
  The mighty tides, whereof its rightful part
Each sea-wide gulf and little weed receiveth—
So, through his soul who earnestly believeth,
  Life from the universal Heart doth flow,
  Whereby some conquest of the eternal wo
By instinct of God's nature he achieveth:
A fuller pulse of this all-powerful Beauty
  Into the poet's gulf-like heart doth tide,
And he more keenly feels the glorious duty
  Of serving Truth despised and crucified—
Happy, unknowing sect or creed, to rest
And feel God flow forever through his breast.

II.

Once hardly in a cycle blossometh
  A flower-like soul ripe with the seeds of song,
  A spirit foreordained to cope with wrong,

Whose divine thoughts are natural as breath,
Who the old Darkness thickly scattereth
   With starry words which shoot prevailing
     light
   Into the deeps, and wither with the blight
Of serene Truth the coward heart of Death :
Wo if such spirit sell his birthright high,
   And mock with lies the longing soul of
     man !
Yet one age longer must true Culture lie,
   Soothing her bitter fetters as she can,
Until new messages of love outstart
At the next beating of the infinite Heart.

III.

The love of all things springs from love of
     one ;
   Wider the soul's horizon hourly grows,
   And over it with fuller glory flows
The sky-like spirit of God ; a hope begun
In doubt and darkness, 'neath a fairer sun
   Cometh to fruitage, if it be of Truth ;
   And to the law of meekness, faith, and ruth,
By inward sympathy shall all be won :
This thou shouldst know, who from the painted
     feature
   Of shifting Fashion, couldst thy brethren
     turn
Unto the love of ever youthful nature,
   And of a beauty fadeless and eterne ;
And always 'tis the saddest sight to see
An old man faithless in Humanity.

IV.

A poet cannot strive for despotism;
  His harp falls shattered; for it still must be
  The instinct of great spirits to be free,
And the sworn foes of cunning barbarism.
He who has deepest searched the wide abysm
  Of that life-giving Soul which men call fate,
  Knows that to put more faith in lies and
      hate
Than truth and love, is the worst atheism:
Upward the soul forever turns her eyes;
  The next hour always shames the hour be-
   fore;
One beauty at its highest prophesies
  That by whose side it shall seem mean and
    poor;
No Godlike thing knows aught of less and less,
But widens to the boundless Perfectness.

V.

Therefore think not the Past is wise alone,
  For Yesterday knows nothing of the Best,
  And thou shalt love it only as the nest
Whence glory-winged things to Heaven have
   flown.
To the great Soul alone are all things known,
  Present and future are to her as past,
  While she in glorious madness doth forecast
That perfect bud which seems a flower full-
  blown
To each new Prophet, and yet always opes
  Fuller and fuller with each day and hour,

Heartening the soul with odor of fresh hopes,
  And longings high and gushings of wide
      power,
Yet never is or shall be fully blown
Save in the forethought of the Eternal One.

VI.

Far 'yond this narrow parapet of Time,
  With eyes uplift, the poet's soul should look
  Into the Endless Promise, nor should brook
One prying doubt to shake his faith sublime;
To him the earth is ever in her prime
  And dewiness of morning; he can see
  Good lying hid, from all eternity,
Within the teeming womb of sin and crime;
His soul shall not be cramped by any bar—
  His nobleness should be so God-like high
That his least deed is perfect as a star,
  His common look majestic as the sky,
And all o'erflooded with a light from far,
Undimmed by clouds of weak mortality.
  Boston April 2, 1842,

THE UNHAPPY LOT OF MR. KNOTT.

PART I.

*Showing how he built his house and his wife moved
into it.*

My worthy friend, A. Gordon Knott,
    From business snug withdrawn,
Was much contented with a lot
Which would contain a Tudor cot
'Twixt twelve feet square of garden-plot,
    And twelve feet more of lawn.

He had laid business on the shelf
    To give his taste expansion,
And, since no man, retired with pelf,
    The building mania can shun,
Knott, being middle-aged himself,
Resolved to build (unhappy elf!)
    A mediæval mansion.

He called an architect in counsel;
    "I want," said he, "a——you know what,
    (You are a builder, I am Knott,)
A thing complete from chimney-pot
Down to the very groundsels;
    Here's a half-acre of good land;
    Just have it nicely mapped and planned

And make your workmen drive on;
  Meadow there is, and upland too,
  And I should like a water-view,
D' you think you could contrive one?
  (Perhaps the pump and trough would do,
  If painted a judicious blue?)
  The woodland I 've attended to ; "
  (He meant three pines stuck up askew,
Two dead ones and a live one.)
  " A pocket-full of rocks 'twould take
To build a house of free-stone,
  But then it is not hard to make
What now-a-days is *the* stone;
  The cunning painter in a trice
  Your house's outside petrifies,
  And people think it very gneiss
Without inquiring deeper;
  My money never shall be thrown
  Away on such a deal of stone,
When stone of deal is cheaper."

And so the greenest of antiques
  Was reared for Knott to dwell in;
The architect worked hard for weeks
In venting all his private peaks
Upon the roof, whose crop of leaks
  Had satisfied Fluellen,
Whatever anybody had
Out of the common, good or bad,
  Knott had it all worked well in,
A donjon-keep, where clothes might dry,
A porter's lodge that was a sty,
A campanile slim and high,

Too small to hang a bell in;
All up and down and here and there,
With Lord-knows-whats of round and square
Stuck on at random everywhere,
It was a house to make one stare,
　All corners and all gables;
Like dogs let loose upon a bear,
Ten emulous styles, *staboyed* with care,
The whole among them seemed to tear,
And all the oddities to spare
　Were set upon the stables.

Knott was delighted with a pile
　Approved by fashion's leaders;
(Only he made the builder smile
By asking every little while,
Why that was called the Twodoor style
　Which certainly had three doors?)
Yet better for this luckless man
If he had put a downright ban
　Upon the thing *in limine;*
For, though to quit affairs his plan,
Ere many days, poor Knott began
Perforce accepting draughts, that ran
　All ways—except up chimney;
The house, though painted stone to mock,
With nice white lines round every block,
　Some trepidation stood in,
When tempests, (with petrific shock,
So to speak) made it really rock,
　Though not a whit less wooden;
And painted stone, howe'er well done,
Will not take in the prodigal sun
　5

Whose beams are never quite at one
　　With our terrestrial lumber ;
So the wood shrank around the knots,
And gaped in disconcerting spots,
And there were lots of dots and rots
　　And crannies without number,
Wherethrough, as you may well presume,
The wind, like water through a flume,
　　Came rushing in ecstatic,
Leaving, in all three floors no room
　　That was not a rheumatic ;
And, what with points and squares and rounds
　　Grown shaky on their poises,
The house at night was full of pounds,
Thumps, bumps, creaks, scratchings, raps—till
　　—" Zounds ! "
Cried Knott, " this goes beyond all bounds,
I do not deal in tongues and sounds,
Nor have I let my house and grounds
　　To a family of Noyeses ! "

But though Knott's house was full of airs,
　　He had but one—a daughter ;
And, as he owned much stocks and shares,
Many who wished to render theirs
Such vain, unsatisfying cares,
And needed wives to sew their tears,
　　In matrimony sought her ;
They vowed her gold they wanted not,
　　Their faith would never falter,
They longed to tie this single Knott
　　In the Hymeneal halter ;
So daily at the door they rang,

Cards for the belle delivering,
Or in the choir at her they sang,
Achieving such a rapturous twang
  As set her nerves a-shivering.

Now Knott had quite made up his mind
  That Colonel Jones should have her;
No beauty he, but oft we find
Sweet kernels 'neath a roughish rind,
So hoped his Jenny 'd be resigned
  And make no more palaver;
Glanced at the fact that love was blind,
That girls were ratherish inclined
  To pet their little crosses,
Then nosologically defined
The rate at which the system pined
In those unfortunates who dined
Upon that metaphoric kind
  Of dish—their own proboscis.

But she with many tears and moans,
  Besought him not to mock her,
Said 'twas too much for flesh and bones,
To marry mortgages and loans,
That father's hearts were stocks and stones
And that she'd go, when Mrs. Jones,
  To Davy Jones's locker;
Then gave her head a little toss
That said as plain as ever was,
If men are always at a loss
  Mere womankind to bridle—
To try the thing on woman cross,
  Were fifty times as idle;

For she a strict resolve had made
    And registered in private,
That either she would die a maid,
Or else be Mrs. Dr. Slade,
    If woman could contrive it;
And, though the wedding-day was set,
    Jenny was more so, rather,
Declaring, in a pretty pet,
That, howsoe'er they spread their net,
She would out Jennyral them yet,
    The colonel and her father.

Just at this time the Public's eyes
    Were keenly on the watch, a stir
Beginning slowly to arise
About those questions and replies,
Those raps that unwrapped mysteries
    So rapidly at Rochester.
And, Knott, already nervous grown
By lying much awake alone,
And listening, sometimes to a moan,
    And sometimes to a clatter,
Whene'er the wind at night would rouse
The ginger-bread-work on his house,
Or when some hasty-tempered mouse,
Behind the plastering, made a towse
    About a family matter,
Began to wonder if his wife,
A paralytic half her life,
    Which made it more surprising,
Might not, to rule him from her urn,
Have taken a peripatetic turn
    For want of exorcising.

This thought, once nestled in his head,
Ere long contagious grew, and spread
Infecting all his mind with dread,
Until at last he lay in bed
And heard his wife, with well-known tread,
Entering the kitchen through the shed,
  (Or was't his fancy mocking?)
Opening the pantry, cutting bread,
And then (she'd been some ten years dead)
  Closets and drawers unlocking;
Or, in his room, (his breath grew thick)
He heard the long familiar click
Of slender needles flying quick,
  As if she knit a stocking;—
For whom?—he prayed that years might
    flit
With pains rheumatic shooting,
Before those ghostly things she knit
Upon his unfleshed sole might fit,
He did not fancy it a bit,
  To stand upon that footing;
At other times, his frightened hairs
  Above the bed-clothes trusting,
He heard her, full of household cares,
(No dream entrapped in supper's snares,
The foal of horrible nightmares,
But broad awake, as he declares,)
Go bustling up and down the stairs,
Or setting back last evening's chairs,
  Or with the poker thrusting
The raked-up sea-coal's hardened crust—
And—what! impossible! it must!
He knew she had returned to dust,

And yet could scarce his senses trust,
Hearing her as she poked and fussed
  About the parlor, dusting!

Night after night he strove to sleep
  And take his ease in spite of it;
But still his flesh would chill and creep,
And, though two night-lamps he might keep,
  He could not so make light of it.
At last, quite desperate, he goes
And tells his neighbors all his woes,
  Which did but their amount enhance;
They made such mockery of his fears,
That soon his days were of all jeers,
  His nights of the rueful countenance;
" I thought most folks," one neighbor said,
" Gave up the ghost when they were dead,"
Another gravely shook his head,
  Adding, " from all we hear, it 's
Quite plain poor Knott is going mad—
For how can he at once be sad
  And think he 's full of spirits?"
A third declared he knew a knife
  Would cut this Knott much quicker,
" The surest way to end all strife,
And lay the spirit of a wife,
  Is just to take and lick her!"
A temperance man caught up the word,
" Ah, yes," he groaned, I 've always heard
  Our poor friend always slanted
Tow'rd taking liquor overmuch;
I fear these spirits may be Dutch,
(A sort of gins, or something such,)

With which his house is haunted;
I see the thing as clear as light—
If Knott would give up getting tight,
  Naught farther would be wanted:"
So all his neighbors stood aloof
And, that the spirits 'neath his roof
Were not entirely up to proof,
  Unanimously granted.

Knott knew that cocks and sprites were foes,
And so bought up, Heaven only knows
How many, though he wanted crows
To give ghosts cause, as I suppose,
  To think that day was breaking;
Moreover, what he called his park,
He turned into a kind of ark,
For dogs, because a little bark
Is a good tonic in the dark,
  If one is given to waking;
But things went on from bad to worse,
His curs were nothing but a curse,
  And, what was still more shocking,
Foul ghosts of living fowl made scoff
And would not think of going off
  In spite of all his cocking.

Shanghais, Bucks-counties, Dominiques,
Malays (that didn't lay for weeks),
  Polanders, Bantams, Dorkings,
Waiving the cost, no trifling ill,
(Since each brought in his little bill)
By day or night were never still,
But every thought of rest would kill

With cacklings and with quorkings;
Henry the Eighth of wives got free
  By a way he had of axing;
But poor Knott's Tudor henery
Was not so fortunate, and he
  Still found his trouble waxing;
As for the dogs, the rows they made,
And how they howled, snarled, barked, **and**
    bayed,
  Beyond all human knowledge is;
All night, as wide awake as gnats,
The terriers rumpused after rats,
Or, just for practice, taught their brats
To worry cast-off shoes and hats,
The bull-dogs settled private spats,
All chased imaginary cats,
Or raved behind the fence's slats
At real ones, or, from their mats,
With friends miles off, held pleasant chats,
Or, like some folks in white cravats,
Contemptuous of sharps and flats,
  Sat up and sang dogsologies.

PART II.

Showing what is meant by a flow of Spirits.

At first the ghosts were somewhat shy,
Coming when none but Knott was nigh,
And people said 'twas all their eye,
(Or rather his) a flam, the sly
  Digestion's machination;
Some recommended a wet sheet,
Some a nice broth of pounded peat,

Some a cold flat-iron to the feet,
Some a decoction of lamb's-bleat;
Some a southwesterly grain of wheat;
Meat was by some pronounced unmeet,
Others thought fish most indiscreet,
And that 't was worse than all to eat
Of vegetables, sour or sweet,
(Except, perhaps, the skin of beet,)
    In such a concatenation :
One quack his button gently plucks
And murmurs " biliary ducks ! "
    Says Knott, " I never ate one ; "
But all, though brimming full of wrath,
Homeo, Allo, Hydropath,
Concurred in this—that t'other's path
    To death's door was the straight one.

But, spite of medical advice,
The ghosts came thicker, and a spice
    Of mischief grew apparent;
Nor did they only come at night,
But seemed to fancy broad daylight,
Till Knott, in horror and affright,
    His unoffending hair rent;
Whene'er, with handkerchief on lap,
He made his elbow-chair a trap
To catch an after-dinner nap,
The spirits, always on the tap,
Would make a sudden *rap, rap, rap,*
The half-spun cord of life to snap,
(And what is life without its nap
But threadbareness and mere mishap ?)
As 't were with a percussion cap

The t· ouble's climax capping;
It seemed a party dried and grim
Of mummies had come to visit him,
Each getting off from every limb
   Its multitudinous wrapping;
Scratchings sometimes the walls ran round,
The merest penny-weights of sound;
Sometimes 't was only by the pound
   They carried on their dealing,
A thumping 'neath the parlor floor
Thump—bump·—thump—bumping o'er and
   o'er,
As if the vegetables in store,
(Quiet and orderly before,)
   Were all together pealing;
You would have thought the thing was done
By the Spirit of some son of a gun,
  And that a forty-two-pounder,
Or that the ghost which made such sounds
Could be none other than John Pounds,
   Of Ragged Schools the founder.

Through three gradations of affright,
The awful noises reached their height;
   At first they knocked nocturnally,
Then, for some reason, changing quite,
(As mourners, after six months' flight,
Turn suddenly from dark to light,)
   Began to knock diurnally,
And last, combining all their stocks,
(Scotland was ne'er so full of Knox,)
Into one Chaos, (father of Nox,)
Nocte pluit—they showered knocks,

And knocked, knocked, knocked eternally;
Ever upon the go, like buoys,
(Wooden sea-urchins,) all Knott's joys,
They turned to trouble and a noise
   That preyed on him internally.

Soon they grew wider in their scope;
Whenever Knott a door would ope,
It would ope not, or else elope
And fly back (curbless as a trope
Once started down a stanza's slope
By a bard that gave it too much rope—)
   Like a clap of thunder slamming;
And, when kind Jenny brought his hat,
(She always, when he walked, did that,)
Just as upon his head it sat,
Submitting to his settling pat—
Some unseen hand would jam it flat,
Or give it such a furious bat
   That eyes and nose went cramming
Up out of sight, and consequently,
As when in life it paddled free,
   His beaver caused much damning;
If these things seem o'erstrained to be,
Read the account of Doctor Dee,
'Tis in our college library;
Read Wesley's circumstantial plea,
And Mrs. Crow, more like a bee,
Sucking the nightshade's honied fee,
And Stilling's Pneumatology;
Consult Scott, Glanvil, grave Wie-
   rus, and both Mathers; further, see

Webster, Casaubon, James First's trea-
  tise, a right royal Q. E. D.
Writ with the moon in perigee,
Bodin de Demonomanie——
(Accent that last line gingerly)
All full of learning as the sea
Of fishes, and all disagree,
Save in *Sathanas apage!*
Or, what will surely put a flea
In unbelieving ears—with glee,
Out of a paper (sent to me
By some friend who forgot to **P** ...
A ... **Y** ...—I use cryptography
Lest I his vengeful pen should dree—
His **P** ... **O** ... **S** ... **T** ... **A** ... **G** ... **E** ..)
    Things to the same effect I cut,
About the tantrums of a ghost,
Not more than three weeks since, at most,
    Near Stratford, in Connecticut.
    [Heavens! what a sentence that is!
    I throw it in, though, gratis,
    And, taking breath, anew
    Catch up my legend's clew.]
Knott's Upas daily spread its roots,
Sent up on all sides livelier shoots,
And bore more pestilential fruits;
The ghosts behaved like downright brutes,
They snipped holes in his Sunday suits,
Practiced all night on octave flutes,
Put peas (not peace) into his boots,
    Whereof grew corns in season,
They scotched his sheets, and, what was worse,
Stuck his silk night-cap full of burs,

Till he, in language plain and terse,
(But much unlike a Bible verse,)
   Swore he should lose his reason.

Of course such doings, far and wide,
With rumors filled the country-side,
And, (as it is our nation's pride,
To think a Truth 's not verified
Till with majorities allied,)
Parties sprung up, affirmed, denied,
And candidates with questions plied,
Who like the circus-riders, tried
At once both hobbies to bestride,
And each with his opponent vied
In being inexplicit.
Earnest inquirers multiplied ;
Folks, whose tenth cousins lately died,
Wrote letters long, and Knott replied ;
All who could either walk or ride,
Gathered to wonder or deride,
   And paid the house a visit ;
Horses were at his pine-trees tied,
Mourners in every corner sighed,
Widows brought children there that cried,
Swarms of lean Seekers, eager-eyed,
(People Knott never could abide,)
Into each hole and cranny pried
With strings of questions cut and dried
From the Devout Inquirer's Guide,
For the wise spirits to decide—
   As, for example, is it
True that the damned are fried or boiled?
Was the Earth's axis greased or oiled?

Who cleaned the moon when it was soiled ?
  How heal diseased potatoes ?
Did spirits have the sense of smell ?
Where would departed spinsters dwell ?
If the late Zenas Smith were well ?
If Earth were solid or a shell ?
Were spirits fond of Doctor Fell ?
Did the bull toll Cock-Robin's knell ?
What remedy would bugs expel ?
If Paine's invention were a sell ?
Did spirits by Webster's system spell ?
Was it a sin to be a belle ?
Did dancing sentence folks to hell ?
If so, then where most torture fell—
  On little toes or great toes ?
If life's true seat were in the brain ?
Did Ensign mean to marry Jane ?
By whom, in fact, was Morgan slain ?
Could matter ever suffer pain ?
What would take out a cherry-stain ?
Who picked the pocket of Seth Crane,
Of Waldo precinct, State of Maine ?
Was Sir John Franklin sought in vain ?
Did primitive Christians over train ?
What was the family-name of Cain ?
Them spoons, were they by Betty ta'en?
Would earth-worm poultice cure a sprain
Was Socrates so dreadful plain ?
What teamster guided Charles's wain ?
Was Uncle Ethan mad or sane ?
And could his will in force remain ?
If not, what counsel to retain ?
Did Le Sage steal Gil Blas from Spain ?

Was Junius writ by Thomas Paine?
Were ducks discomforted by rain?
How did Britannia rule the main?
Was Jonas coming back again?
Was vital truth upon the wane?
Did ghosts, to scare folks, drag a chain?
Who was our Huldah's chosen swain?
Did none have teeth pulled without payin',
   Ere ether was invented?
Whether mankind would not agree,
If the universe were tuned in C?
What was it ailed Lucindy's knee?
Whether folks eat folks in Feejee?
Whether *his* name would end with T?
If Saturn's rings were two or three?
And what bump in Phrenology
   They truely represented?
These problems dark, wherein they groped,
Wherewith man's reason vainly coped,
Now that the spirit-world was oped,
In all humility they hoped
   Would be resolved *instanter ;*
Each of the miscellaneous rout
Brought his, or her, own little doubt,
And wished to pump the spirits out,
Through his, or her, own private spout,
   Into his, or her, decanter.

PART III.

Wherein it is shown that the most ardent Spirits are
more ornamental than useful.

Many a speculating wight
Came by express-trains, day and night,
To see if Knott would " sell his right,"
Meaning to make the ghosts a sight—
　　What they called a " meenaygerie; "
One threatened, if he would not " trade,"
His run of custom to invade,
(He could not these sharp folks persuade
That he was not, in some way, paid,)
　　And stamp him as a plagiary,
By coming down, at one fell swoop,
With THE ORIGINAL KNOCKING TROUPE,
　　Come recently from Hades,
Who (for a quarter-dollar heard)
Would ne'er rap out a hasty word
Whence any blame might be incurred
　　From the most fastidious ladies;
The late lamented Jesse Soule
To stir the ghosts up with a pole
And be director of the whole,
　　Who was engaged the rather
For the rare merits he 'd combine,
Having been in the spirit line,
Which trade he only did resign
With general applause, to shine,
Awful in mail of cotton fine,
　　As ghost of Hamlet's father!
Another a fair plan reveals
Never yet hit on, which, he feels,

To Knott's religious sense appeals—
" We 'll have your house set up on wheels,
    A speculation pious ;
For music we can shortly find
A barrel-organ that will grind
Psalm-tunes (an instrument designed
For the New England tour) refined
From secular drosses, and inclined
To an unworldly turn (combined
    With no sectarian bias ;)
Then, traveling by stages slow,
Under the style of Knott & Co.,
I would accompany the show
As moral lecturer, the foe
Of Rationalism ; you could throw
The rappings in, and make them go
Strict Puritan principles, you know,
(How *do* you make 'em ? with your toe ?)
And the receipts which thence might flow,
    We could divide between us ;
Still more attractions to combine,
Beside these services of mine,
I will throw in a very fine
(It would do nicely for a sign)
    Original Titian's Venus."
Another offered handsome fees
If Knott would get Demosthenes.
(Nay, his mere knuckles, for more ease,)
To rap a few short sentences ;
Or if, for want of proper keys,
    His Greek might make confusion,
Then, just to get a rap from Burke,
To recommend a little work
    6

On Public Elocution.
(*Nonnulla hîc desnut
Meliora quae sunt.*)

Meanwhile the spirits made replies
To all the reverent *whats* and *whys*,
Resolving doubts of every size,
And giving seekers grave and wise,
Who came to know their destinies,
  A rap-turous reception ;
When unbelievers void of grace
Came to investigate the place,
(Creatures of Sadducistic race,
With groveling intellects and base)
They could not find the slightest trace
  To indicate deception ;
Indeed, it is declared by some
That spirits (of this sort) are glum,
Almost, or wholly, deaf and dumb,
And (out of self-respect) quite mum
To sceptic natures cold and numb,
Who of *this* kind of Kingdom Come,
  Have not a just conception ;
True, there were people who demurred
That, though the raps no doubt were heard
  Both under them and o'er them,
Yet, somehow, when a search they made,
They found Miss Jenny sore afraid,
Or Jenny's lover, Doctor Slade,
Equally awe-struck and dismayed,
Or Deborah, the chamber-maid,
Whose terrors, not to be gainsaid,
In laughs hysteric were displayed,

Was always there before them;
This had its due effect with some
Who straight departed, muttering, **Hum!**
Transparent hoax! and Gammon!
But these were few; believing souls
Came, day by day, in larger shoals,
As, the ancients to the windy holes
'Neath Delphi's tripod brought their **doles,**
Or to the shrine of Ammon.
The spirits seemed exceeding tame,
Call whom you fancied and he came;
The shades august of eldest fame
You summoned with an awful ease;
As grosser spirits gurgled out
From chair and table with a spout,
In Auerbach's cellar once, to flout
The senses of the rabble rout,
Where'er the gimlet twirled about
Of cunning Mephistophiles—
So did these spirits seem in store,
Behind the wainscot or the door,
Ready to thrill the being's core
Of every enterprising bore
With their astounding glamour;
Whatever ghost one wished to hear,
By strange coincidence, was near
To make the past or future clear,
(Sometimes in shocking grammar,)
By raps and taps, now there, now here—
It seemed as if the spirit queer
Of some departed auctioneer
Were doomed to practice by the **year**
With the spirit of his hammer;

Whate'er you asked was answered, yet
One could not very deeply get
Into the obliging spirits' debt,
Because they used the alphabet
   In all communications,
And new revealings (though sublime)
Rapped out, one letter at a time,
   With boggles, hesitations,
Stoppings, beginnings o'er again,
And getting matters into train,
Could hardly overload the brain
   With too excessive rations,
Since just to ask *if two and two
Really make four?* or, *How d' ye do?*
And get the fit replies thereto
In the tramundane rat-tat-too,
   Might ask a whole day's patience.

'T was strange ('mongst other things) to find
In what odd sets the ghosts combined,
   Happy forthwith to thump any
Piece of intelligence inspired,
The truth whereof had been inquired
   By some one of the company;
For instance, Fielding, Mirabeau,
Orator Henley, Cicero,
Paley, John Zisca, Marivaux,
Melancthon, Robertson, Junot,
Scaliger, Chesterfield, Rousseau,
Hakluyt, Boccaccio, South, De Foe,
Diaz, Josephus, Richard Roe,
Odin, Arminius, Charles *le gros*,
Tiresias, the late James Crow,

Casabianca, Grose, Prideaux,
Old Grimes, Young Norval, Swift, Brissot,
Maimonides, the Chevalier D 'O,
Socrates, Fenelon, Job, Stow,
The inventor of *Elixir pro*,
Euripides, Spinoza, Poe,
Confucius, Hiram Smith, and Fo,
Came (as it seemed, somewhat *de trop*)
With a disembodied Esquimaux,
To say that it was so and so,
   With Franklin's Expedition;
One testified to ice and snow,
One that the mercury was low,
One that his progress was quite slow,
One that he much desired to go,
One that the cook had frozen his toe,
(Dissented from by Dandolo,
Wordsworth, Cynaegirus, Boileau,
La Hontan and Sir Thomas Roe,)
One saw twelve white bears in a row,
One saw eleven and a crow,
With other things we could not know
(Of great statistic value, though)
   By our mere mortal vision,
Sometimes the spirits made mistakes,
And seemed to play at ducks and drakes,
With bold inquiry's heaviest stakes
   In science or in mystery;
They knew so little (and that wrong)
Yet rapped it out so bold and strong,
One would have said the entire throng
   Had been Professors of History;
What made it odder was, that those

Who, you would naturally suppose,
Could solve a question, if they chose,
As easily as count their toes
   Were just the ones that blundered;
One day, Ulysses happening down,
A reader of Sir Thomas Browne
   And who (with him) had wondered
What song it was the Sirens sang,
Asked the shrewd Ithacan—*bang! bang!*
With this response the chamber rang,
   "I guess it was Old Hundred."
And Franklin, being asked to name
The reason why the lightning came,
   Replied, " Because it thundered."

On one sole point the ghosts agreed,
One fearful point, than which, indeed,
   Nothing could seem absurder ;
Poor Colonel Jones they all abused,
And finally downright accused
   The poor old man of murder ;
'Twas thus ; by dreadful raps was shown
Some spirit's longing to make known
A bloody fact, which he alone
Was privy to, (such ghosts more prone
   In Earth's affairs to meddle are;)
Who are you? with awe-stricken looks,
All ask : his airy knuckles he crooks,
And raps, " I *was* Eliab Snooks,
   That used to be a pedler;
Some on ye still are on my books ! "
Whereat, to inconspicuous nooks,
(More fearing this than common spooks,)

Shrank each indebted meddler;
Further the vengeful ghost declared
That while his earthly life was spared,
About the country he had fared,
    A duly licensed follower
Of that much-wandering trade that wins
Slow profit from the sale of tins,
    And various kinds of hollow-ware;
That Colonel Jones enticed him in
Pretending that he wanted tin,
There slew him with a rolling-pin,
Hid him in a potato-bin,
    And (the same night) him ferried
Across Great Pond to t'other shore,
And there on land of Widow Moore,
Just where you turn to Larkin's store,
    Under a rock him buried;
Some friends (who happened to be by)
He called upon to testify
That what he said was not a lie,
    And that he did not stir this
Foul matter out of any spite
But from a simple love of right;—
    Which statement the Nine Worthies,
Rabbi Akiba, Charlemagne,
Seth, Colley Cibber, General Wayne,
Cambyses, Tasso, Tubal-Cain,
The owner of a castle in Spain,
Jehangire, and the Widow of Nain,
(The friends aforesaid) made more plain
    And by loud raps attested;
To the same purport testified
Plato, John Wilkes, and Colonel Pride

Who knew said Snooks before he died,
  Had in his wares invested,
Thought him entitled to belief
And freely could concur, in brief
    In every thing the rest did.

Eliab this occasion seized,
(Distinctly here the Spirit sneezed)
To say that he should ne'er be eased
Till Jenny married whom she pleased,
  Free from all checks and urgin's
(This spirit dropped his final g's,)
And that, unless Knott quickly sees
This done, the spirits to appease,
They would come back his life to tease
As thick as mites in ancient cheese,
And let his house on an endless lease
To the ghosts (terrific rappers these
And veritable Eumenides,)
  Of the Eleven Thousand Virgins!

Knott was perplexed and shook his head,
He did not wish his child to wed
  With a suspected murderer,
(For, true or false, the rumor spread,)
But as for this riled life he led,
" It would not answer," so he said,
  " To have it go no furderer."

At last, scarce knowing what it meant,
Reluctantly he gave consent
That Jenny, since 't was evident
That she *would* follow her own bent,

Should make her own election;
For that appeared the only way
These frightful noises to allay
Which had already turned him gray
  And plunged him in dejection.

Accordingly, this artless maid
Her father's ordinance obeyed,
And, all in whitest crape arrayed,
(Miss Pulsifer the dresses made
And wishes here the fact displayed
That she still carries on the trade,
The third door south from Bagg's Arcade,)
A very faint "I do" essayed
And gave her hand to Hiram Slade,
From which time forth, the ghosts were laid;
  And ne'er gave trouble after;
But the Selectmen, be it known,
Dug underneath the aforesaid stone,
Where the poor pedler's corpse was thrown,
And found there-under a jaw-bone,
Though, when the crowner sat thereon,
He nothing hatched, except alone
  Successive broods of laughter;
It was a frail and dingy thing,
In which a grinder or two did cling,
  In color like molasses,
Which surgeons, called from far and wide,
Upon the horror to decide,
  Having put on their glasses,
Reported thus—"To judge by looks,
These bones, by some queer hooks or crooks,
May have belonged to Mr. Snooks,

But, as men deepest read in books
   Are perfectly aware, bones,
If buried, fifty years or so,
Lose their identity and grow
   From human bones to bare bones."

Still, if to Jaalam you go down,
You'll find two parties in the town,
One headed by Benaiah Brown,
   And one by Perez Tinkham;
The first believe the ghosts all through,
And vow that they shall never rue
The happy chance by which they knew
That people in Jupiter are blue,
And very fond of Irish stew,
Two curious facts when Prince Lee Boo
Rapped clearly to a chosen few—
   Whereas the others think 'em
A trick got up by Doctor Slade
With Deborah the chamber-maid
   And that sly cretur Jenny,
That all the revelations wise,
At which the Brownites made big eyes,
Might have been given by Jared Keyes,
   A natural fool and ninny.
And, last week, didn't Eliab Snooks,
Come back with never better looks,
As sharp as new bought mackerel hooks,
And bright as a new pin, eh?
Good Parson Wilbur, too, avers
(Though to be mixed in parish stirs
Is worse than handling chestnut-burs)
That no case to his mind occurs

Where spirits ever did converse
Save in a kind of guttural Erse,
  (So say the best authorities ;)
And that a charge by raps conveyed,
Should be most scrupulously weighed
  And searched into before it is
Made public, since it may give pain
That cannot soon be cured again,
And one word may infix a stain
  Which ten cannot gloss over,
Though speaking for his private part,
He is rejoiced with all his heart
  Miss Knott missed not her lover
December, 1850.

HAKON'S LAY.

Then Thorstein looked at Hakon, where he sate,
Mute as a cloud amid the stormy hall,
And said : " O, Skald, sing now an olden song,
Such as our fathers heard who led great lives ;
And, as the bravest on a shield is borne
Along the waving host that shouts him king,
So rode their thrones upon the thronging seas ! "

Then the old man arose, white-haired he stood,
White-bearded, and with eyes that looked afar
From their still region of perpetual snow,
Over the little smokes and stirs of men :
His head was bowed with gathered flakes of
    years,

As winter bends the sea-foreboding pine
But something triumphed in his brow and eye,
Which whoso saw it, could not see and crouch:
Loud rang the emptied beakers as he mused,
Brooding his eyried thoughts ; then, as an eagle
Circles smooth-winged above the wind-vexed
    woods,
So wheeled his soul into the air of song
High o'er the stormy hall; and thus he sang:

" The fletcher for his arrow-shaft picks out
Wood closest-grained, long-seasoned, straight
    as light;
And, from a quiver full of such as these,
The wary bow-man, matched against his peers,
Long doubting, singles yet once more the best.
Who is it that can make such shafts as Fate?
What archer of his arrows is so choice,
Or hits the white so surely?   They are men,
The chosen of her quiver; nor for her
Will every reed suffice, or cross-grained stick
At random from life's vulgar fagot plucked :
Such answer household ends ; but she will have
Souls straight and clear, of toughest fibre, sound
Down to the heart of heart; from these she
    strips
All needless stuff, all sapwood, hardens them,
From circumstance untoward feathers plucks
Crumpled and cheap, and barbs with iron will :
The hour that passes is her quiver-boy ;
When she draws bow, 'tis not across the wind,
Nor 'gainst the sun, her haste-snatched arrow
    sings,

For sun and wind have plighted faith to her :
Ere men have heard the sinew twang, behold,
In the butt's heart her trembling messenger !

" The song is old and simple that I sing :
Good were the days of yore, when men were
        tried
By ring of shields, as now by ring of gold ;
But, while the gods are left, and hearts of men,
And the free ocean, still the days are good ;
Through the broad Earth roams Opportunity
And knocks at every door of hut or hall,
Until she finds the brave soul that she wants."

He ceased, and instantly the frothy tide
Of interrupted wassail roared along ;
But Leif, the son of Eric, sate apart
Musing, and, with his eyes upon the fire,
Saw shapes of arrows, lost as soon as seen ;
But then with that resolve his heart was bent,
Which, like a humming shaft, through many
        a strife
Of day and night across the unventured seas,
Shot the brave prow to cut on Vinland sands
The first rune in the Saga of the West.

TO THE FUTURE.

O, Land of Promise! from what Pisgah's
    height
  Can I behold thy stretch of peaceful bowers?
Thy golden harvests flowing out of sight,
    Thy nestled homes and sun-illumined towers
Gazing upon the sunset's high-heaped gold,
  Its crags of opal and of chrysolite,
Its deeps on deeps of glory that unfold
    Still brightening abysses,
    And blazing precipices,
Whence but a scanty leap it seems to heaven,
    Sometimes a glimpse is given,
Of thy more gorgeous realm, thy more un-
    stinted blisses.

O, Land of Quiet! to thy shore the surf
  Of the perturbed Present rolls and sleeps;
Our storms breathe soft as June upon thy turf
  And lure out blossoms; to thy bosom leaps,
As to a mother's, the o'er wearied heart,
Hearing far off and dim the toiling mart,
    The hurrying feet, the curses without
      number.
    And, circled with the glow Elysian,
    Of thine exulting vision,
Out of its very cares wooes charms for peace
    and slumber.

To thee the Earth lifts up her fettered hands
   And cries for vengeance; with a pitying
     smile
Thou blessest her, and she forgets her bands,
   And her old wo-worn face a little while
Grows young and noble; unto thee the Op-
   pressor
     Looks, and is dumb with awe;
     The eternal law
Which makes the crime its own blindfold
   redresser,
   Shadows his heart with perilous foreboding,
     And he can see the grim-eyed Doom
     From out the trembling gloom
Its silent-footed steeds toward his palace
   goading.

What promises hast thou for Poet's eyes,
   Aweary of the turmoil and the wrong!
To all their hopes what over-joyed replies!
   What undreamed ecstasies for blissful song!
Thy happy plains no war-trump's brawling
   clangor
   Disturbs, and fools the poor to hate the poor;
The humble glares not on the high with anger;
   Love leaves no grudge at less, no greed for
     more;
In vain strives Self the godlike sense to
   smother.
     From the soul's deeps
     It throbs and leaps;
The noble 'neath foul rags beholds his long-
   lost brother.

To thee the Martyr looketh, and his fires
   Unlock their fangs and leave his spirit free;
To thee the Poet 'mid his toil aspires,
   And grief and hunger climb about his knee
Welcome as children; thou upholdest
   The lone Inventor by his demon haunted;
The Prophet cries to thee when hearts are
      coldest,
     And, gazing o'er the midnight's bleak abyss,
     Sees the drowsed soul awaken at thy kiss,
And stretch its happy arms and leap up dis-
      enchanted.

Thou bringest vengeance, but so loving kindly
   The guilty thinks it pity; taught by thee
Fierce tyrants drop the scourges wherewith
      blindly
   Their own souls they were scarring; con-
      querors see
With horror in their hands the accursed spear
   That tore the meek One's side on Calvary,
And from their trophies shrink with ghastly
      fear;
   Thou, too, art the Forgiver,
The beauty of man's soul to man revealing;
   The arrows from thy quiver
Pierce error's guilty heart, but only pierce for
      healing,

O, whither, whither, glory-winged dreams,
   From out Life's sweat and turmoil would y
      bear me?
Shut, gates of Fancy, on your golden gleams,

This agony of hopeless contrast spare me!
Fade, cheating glow, and leave me to my night!
　　He is a coward who would borrow
　　A charm against the present sorrow
From the vague Future's promise of delight:
　　As life's alarums nearer roll,
　　　The ancestral buckler calls,
　　　Self-clanging, from the walls
　　In the high temple of the soul;
Where are most sorrows, there the poet's
　　　sphere is,
　　　To feed the soul with patience,
　　　To heal its desolations
With words of unshorn truth, with love that
　　　never wearies.

OUT OF DOORS.

'Tis good to be abroad in the sun,
His gifts abide when day is done;
Each thing in nature from his cup
Gathers a several virtue up;
The grace within its being's reach
Becomes the nutriment of each,
And the same life imbibed by all
Makes each most individual:
Here the twig-bending peaches seek
The glow that mantles in their cheek—
Hence comes the Indian-Summer bloom
That hazes round the basking plum,
And, from the same impartial light,
The grass sucks green, the lily white.
　7

Like these the soul, for sunshine made,
Grows wan and gracile in the shade,
Her faculties, which God decreed
Various as Summer's dædal breed,
With one sad color are imbued,
Shut from the sun that tints their **blood;**
The shadow of the poet's roof
Deadens the dyes of warp and woof;
Whate'er of ancient song remains
Has fresh air flowing in its veins,
For Greece and eldest Ind knew well
That out of doors, with world-wide **swell**
Arches the student's lawful cell.

Away, unfruitful lore of books,
For whose vain idiom we reject
The spirit's mother-dialect,
Aliens among the birds and brooks,
Dull to interpret or believe
What gospels lost the woods retrieve,
Or what the eaves-dropping violet
Reports from God, who walketh yet
His garden in the hush of eve!
Away, ye pedants city-bred,
Unwise of heart, too wise of head,
Who handcuff Art with *thus* and *so*,
And in each other's footprints tread,
Like those who walk through drifted **snow;**

Who, from deep study of brick walls,
Conjecture of the water-falls,
By six square feet of smoke-stained **sky**
Compute those deeps that overlie

The still tarn's heaven-anointed eye,
And, in your earthen crucible,
With chemic tests essay to spell
How nature works in field and dell!
Seek we where Shakspeare buried gold?
Such hands no charmed witch-hazel hold;
To beach and rock repeats the sea
The mystic *Open Sesame ;*
Old Greylock's voices not in vain
Comment on Milton's mountain strain,
And cunningly the various wind
Spenser's locked music can unbind.

A REVERIE.

In the twilight deep and silent
Comes thy spirit unto mine,
When the moonlight and the starlight
Over cliff and woodland shine,
And the quiver of the river
Seems a thrill of joy benign.

Then I rise and wander slowly
To the headland by the sea,
When the evening star throbs setting
Through the cloudy cedar tree,
And from under, mellow thunder
Of the surf comes fitfully.

Then within my soul I feel thee
Like a gleam of other years,

Visions of my childhood murmur
Their old madness in my ears,
Till the pleasance of thy presence
Cools my heart with blissful tears.

All the wondrous dreams of boyhood—
All youth's fiery thirst of praise—
All the surer hopes of manhood
Blossoming in sadder days—
Joys that bound me, griefs that crowned me
With a better wreath than bays—

All the longings after freedom—
The vague love of human kind,
Wandering far and near at random
Like a winged seed in the wind—
The dim yearnings and fierce burnings
Of an undirected mind—

All of these, oh best beloved,
Happiest present dreams and past,
In thy love find safe fulfillment,
Ripened into truths at last;
Faith and beauty, hope and duty,
To one centre gather fast.

How my nature, like an ocean,
At the breath of thine awakes,
Leaps its shores in mad exulting
And in foamy thunder breaks,
Then downsinking, lieth shrinking
At the tumult that it makes !

Blazing Hesperus hath sunken
Low within the pale-blue west,
And with golden splendor crowneth
The horizon's piny crest;
Thoughtful quiet stills the riot
Of wild longing in my breast.

Home I loiter through the moonlight,
Underneath the quivering trees,
Which, as if a spirit stirred them,
Sway and bend, till by degrees
The far surge's murmur merges
In the rustle of the breeze.

IN SADNESS.

There is not in this life of ours
  One bliss unmixed with fears,
The hope that wakes our deepest powers
  A face of sadness wears,
And the dew that showers our dearest flowers
  Is the bitter dew of tears.

Fame waiteth long, and lingereth
  Through weary nights and morns—
And evermore the shadow Death
  With mocking finger scorns
That underneath the laurel wreath
  Should be a wreath of thorns.

The laurel leaves are cool and green,
  But the thorns are hot and sharp,

Lean Hunger grins and stares between
  The poet and his harp,
Though of Love's sunny sheen his woof have
   · been
  Grim want thrusts in the warp.

And if beyond this darksome clime
  Some fair star Hope may see,
That keeps unjarred the blissful chime
  Of its golden infancy—
Where the harvest-time of faith sublime
  Not always is to be—

Yet would the true soul rather choose
  Its home where sorrow is,
Than in a stated peace to lose
  Its life's supremest bliss—
The rainbow hues that bend profuse
  O'er cloudy spheres like this—

The want, the sorrow and the pain,
  That are Love's right to cure—
The sunshine bursting after rain—
  The gladness insecure
That makes us fain strong hearts to gain,
  To do and to endure.

High natures must be thunder-scarred
  With many a searing wrong;
From mother Sorrow's breasts the bard
  Sucks gifts of deepest song,
Nor all unmarred with struggles hard
  Wax the Soul's sinews strong.

Dear Patience, too, is born of wo,
  Patience that opes the gate
Wherethrough the soul of man must go
  Up to each nobler state,
Whose voice's flow so meek and low
  Smooths the bent brows of Fate.

Though Fame be slow, yet Death is swift,
  And, o'er the spirit's eyes,
Life after life doth change and shift
  With larger destinies:
As on we drift, some wider rift
  Shows us serener skies.

And though naught falleth to us here
  But gains the world counts loss,
Though all we hope of wisdom clear
  When climbed to seems but dross,
Yet all, though ne'er Christ's faith they **wear,**
  At least may share his cross.

FAREWELL.

FAREWELL! as the bee round the blossom
Doth murmur drowsily,
So murmureth round my bosom
The memory of thee;
Lingering, it seems to go,
When the wind more full doth flow,
Waving the flower to and fro,
But still returneth, Marian!

My hope no longer burneth,
Which did so fiercely burn,
My joy to sorrow turneth,
Although loath, loath to turn—
I would forget—
And yet—and yet
My heart to thee still yearneth, Marian!
Fair as a single star thou shinest,
And white as lilies are
The slender hands wherewith thou twinest
Thy heavy auburn hair;
Thou art to me
A memory
Of all that is divinest:
Thou art so fair and tall,
Thy looks so queenly are,
Thy very shadow on the wall,
Thy step upon the stair,
The thought that thou art nigh,
The chance look of thine eye
Are more to me than all, Marian,
And will be till I die!

As the last quiver of a bell
Doth fade into the air,
With a subsiding swell
That dies we know not where,
So my hope melted and was gone:
I raised mine eyes to bless the star
That shared its light with me so far
Below its silver throne,
And gloom and chilling vacancy
Were all was left to me,

In the dark, bleak, night I was alone!
Alone in the blessed Earth, Marian,
For what were all to me—
Its love, and light, and mirth, Marian,
If I were not with thee?

My heart will not forget thee
More than the moaning brine
Forgets the moon when she is set.
The gush when first I met thee
That thrilled my brain like wine,
Doth thrill as madly yet;
My heart cannot forget thee,
Though it may droop and pine,
Too deeply it had set thee
In every love of mine;
No new moon ever cometh,
No flower ever bloometh,
No twilight ever gloometh
But I'm more only thine.
Oh look not on me, Marian,
Thine eyes are wild and deep,
And they have won me, Marian,
From peacefulness and sleep;
The sunlight doth not sun me,
The meek moonshine doth shun me,
All sweetest voices stun me—
There is no rest
Within my breast
And I can only weep, Marian!

As a landbird far at sea
Doth wander through the sleet

And drooping downward wearily
Finds no rest for her feet,
So wandereth my memory
O'er the years when we did meet:
I used to say that everything
Partook a share of thee,
That not a little bird could sing,
Or green leaf flutter on a tree,
That nothing could be beautiful
Save part of thee were there,
That from thy soul so clear and full
All bright and blessed things did cull
The charm to make them fair;
And now I know
That it was so,
Thy spirit through the earth doth flow
And face me wheresoe'er I go—
What right hath perfectness to give
Such weary weight of wo
Unto the soul which cannot live
On anything more low?
Oh leave me, leave me, Marian,
There's no fair thing I see
But doth deceive me, Marian,
Into sad dreams of thee!
A cold snake gnaws my heart
And crushes round my brain,
And I should glory but to part
So bitterly again,
Feeling the slow tears start
And fall in fiery rain:
There's a wide ring round the moon,
The ghost-like clouds glide by,

And I hear the sad winds croon
A dirge to the lowering sky;
There's nothing soft or mild
In the pale moon's sickly light,
But all looks strange and wild
Through the dim, foreboding night:
I think thou must be dead
In some dark and lonely place,
With candles at thy head,
And a pall above thee spread
To hide thy dead, cold face;
But I can see thee underneath
So pale, and still, and fair,
Thine eyes closed smoothly and a wreath
Of flowers in thy hair;
I never saw thy face so clear
When thou wast with the living,
As now beneath the pall, so drear,
And stiff, and unforgiving;
I cannot flee thee, Marian,
I cannot turn away,
Mine eyes must see thee, Marian,
Through salt tears night and day.

A DIRGE.

POET! lonely is thy bed,
And the turf is overhead—
  Cold earth is thy cover;
But thy heart hath found release,
And it slumbers full of peace

'Neath the rustle of green trees
And the warm hum of the bees,
  'Mid the drowsy clover;
Through thy chamber, still as death,
A smooth gurgle wandereth,
As the blue stream murmureth
  To the blue sky over.

Three paces from the silver strand,
Gently in the fine, white sand,
With a lily in thy hand,
  Pale as snow, they laid thee;
In no coarse earth wast thou hid,
And no gloomy coffin-lid
Darkly overweighed thee.
Silently as snow-flakes drift,
The smooth sand did sift and sift
  O'er the bed they made thee;
All sweet birds did come and sing
At thy sunny burying—
  Choristers unbidden,
And, beloved of sun and dew.
Meek forget-me-nots upgrew
Where thine eyes so large and blue
  'Neath the turf were hidden.

Where thy stainless clay doth lie,
Blue and open is the sky,
And the white clouds wander by,
Dreams of summer silently
  Darkening the river;
Thou hearest the clear water run;
And the ripples every one,

Scattering the golden sun,
  Though thy silence quiver;
Vines trail down upon the stream,
Into its smooth and glassy dream
  A green stillness spreading,
And the shiner, perch, and bream
Through the shadowed waters gleam
  'Gainst the current heading.

White as snow, thy winding sheet
Shelters thee from head to feet,
  Save thy pale face only;
Thy face is turned toward the skies,
The lids lie meekly o'er thine eyes,
And the low-voiced pine-tree sighs
  O'er thy bed so lonely.
All thy life thou lov'dst its shade:
Underneath it thou art laid,
  In an endless she'ter;
Thou hearest it forever sigh
As the wind's vague longings die
In its branches dim and high—
Thou hear'st the waters gliding by
  Slumberously welter.

Thou wast full of love and truth,
Of forgivingness and ruth—
Thy great heart with hope and youth
  Tided to o'erflowing.
Thou didst dwell in mysteries,
And there lingered on thine eyes
Shadows of serener skies,
Awfully wild memories,

That were like foreknowing;
Through the earth thou would'st have gone,
Lighted from within alone,
Seeds from flowers in Heaven grown
 With a free hand sowing.

Thou didst remember well and long
Some fragments of thine angel-song,
And strive, through want and wo and wrong
 To win the world unto it;
Thy sin it was to see and hear
Beyond To-day's dim hemisphere—
Beyond all mists of hope and fear,
Into a life more true and clear,
 And dearly thou didst rue it;
Light of the new world thou hadst won,
O'erflooded by a purer sun—
Slowly Fate's ship came drifting on,
And through the dark, save thou, not one
 Caught of the land a token.
Thou stood'st upon the farthest prow,
Something within thy soul said " Now! "
And leaping forth with eager brow,
 Thou fell'st on shore heart-broken.

Long time thy brethren stood in fear;
Only the breakers far and near,
White with their anger, they could hear;
The sounds of land, which thy quick ear
 Caught long ago, they heard not.
And, when at last they reached the strand,
They found thee lying on the sand
With some wild flowers in thy hand,

But thy cold bosom stirred not;
They listened, but they heard no sound
Save from the glad life all around
   A low, contented murmur.
The long grass flowed adown the hill.
A hum rose from a hidden rill,
But thy glad heart, that knew no ill
But too much love, lay dead and still—
The only thing that sent a chill
   Into the heart of summer.

Thou didst not seek the poet's wreath
   But too soon didst win it;
Without 'twas green, but underneath
Were scorn and loneliness and death,
Gnawing the brain with burning teeth,
   And making mock within it.
Thou, who wast full of nobleness,
Whose very life-blood 'twas to bless,
   Whose soul's one law was giving,
Must bandy words with wickedness,
Haggle with hunger and distress,
To win that death which worldliness
   Calls bitterly a living.

"Thou sow'st no gold, and shalt not reap!"
Muttered earth, turning in her sleep;
"Come home to the Eternal Deep!"
Murmured a voice, and a wide sweep
Of wings through thy soul's hush did creep,
   As of thy doom o'erflying;
It seem'd that thy strong heart would leap
Out of thy breast, and thou didst weep,

But not with fear of dying;
Men could not fathom thy deep fears,
They could not understand thy tears,
The hoarded agony of years
    Of bitter self-denying.
So once, when high above the spheres
Thy spirit sought its starry peers,
It came not back to face the jeers
    Of brothers who denied it;
Star-crowned, thou dost possess the deeps
Of God, and thy white body sleeps
Where the lone pine forever keeps
Patient watch beside it.

Poet! underneath the turf,
    Soft thou sleepest, free from morrow,
Thou hast struggled through the surf
    Of wild thoughts and want and sorrow.
Now, beneath the moaning pine,
    Full of rest, thy body lieth,
While far up is clear sunshine,
Underneath a sky divine,
    Her loosed wings thy spirit trieth
Oft she strove to spread them here
But they were too white and clear
    For our dingy atmosphere.

Thy body findeth ample room
In its still and grassy tomb
    By the silent river;
But thy spirit found the earth
Narrow for the mighty birth
    Which it dreamed of ever;

Thou wast guilty of a rhyme
Learned in a benigner clime,
And of that more grievous crime,
An ideal too sublime
For the low-hung sky of Time.

The calm spot where thy body lies
Gladdens thy soul in Paradise,
   It is so still and holy;
Thy body sleeps serenely there,
And well for it thy soul may care,
It was so beautiful and fair,
   Lily white so wholly.

From so pure and sweet a frame
Thy spirit parted as it came,
   Gentle as a maiden;
Now it lieth full of rest—
Sods are lighter on its breast
Than the great, prophetic guest
   Wherewith it was laden.

FANCIES ABOUT A ROSEBUD,

PRESSED IN AN OLD COPY OF SPENSER.

Who prest you here?   The Past can tell,
  When summer skies were bright above,
And some full heart did leap and swell
  Beneath the white new moon of love.
  8

Some Poet, haply, when th. world
  Showed like a calm sea, grand and blue,
Ere its cold, inky waves had curled
  O'er the numb heart once warm and true;

When, with his soul brimful of morn,
  He looked beyond the vale of Time,
Nor saw therein the dullard scorn
  That made his heavenliness a crime;

When, musing o'er the Poets olden,
  His soul did like a sun upstart
To shoot its arrows, clear and golden,
  Through slavery's cold and darksome heart.

Alas! too soon the veil is lifted
  That hangs between the soul and pain,
Too soon the morning-red hath drifted
  Into dull cloud, or fallen in rain!

Or were you prest by one who nurst
  Bleak memories of love gone by,
Whose heart, like a star fallen, burst
  In dark and erring vacancy?

To him you still were fresh and green
  As when you grew upon the stalk,
And many a breezy summer scene
  Came back—and many a moonlit walk;

And there would be a hum of bees,
  A smell of childhood in the air,
And old, fresh feelings cooled the breeze
  That, like loved fingers, stirred his hair!

Then would you suddenly be blasted
  By the keen wind of one dark thought,
One nameless woe, that had outlasted
  The sudden blow whereby 'twas brought.

Or were you pressed here by two lovers
  Who seemed to read these verses rare,
But found between the antique covers
  What Spenser could not prison there:

Songs which his glorious soul had heard,
  But his dull pen could never write,
Which flew, like some gold-winged bird,
  Through the blue heaven out of sight?

My heart is with them as they sit,
  I see the rosebud in her breast,
I see her small hand taking it
  From out its odorous, snowy nest;

I hear him swear that he will keep it,
  In memory of that blessed day,
To smile on it or over-weep it
  When she and spring are far away.

Ah me! I needs must droop my head,
  And brush away a happy tear,
For they are gone, and, dry and dead,
  The rosebud lies before me here.

Yet is it in no stranger's hand,
  For I will guard it tenderly,
And it shall be a magic wand
  To bring mine own true love to me.

My heart runs o'er with sweet surmises,
  The while my fancy weaves her rhyme,
Kind hopes and musical surprises
  Throng round me from the olden time.

I do not care to know who prest you :
  Enough for me to feel and know
That some heart's love and longing blest you,
  Knitting to-day with long-ago.

NEW YEAR'S EVE, 1844.

A FRAGMENT.

THE night is calm and beautiful ; the snow
Sparkles beneath the clear and frosty moon
And the cold stars, as if it took delight
In its own silent whiteness ; the hushed earth
Sleeps in the soft arms of the embracing blue,
Secure as if angelic squadrons yet
Encamped about her, and each watching star
Gained double brightness from the flashing
    arms
Of winged and unsleeping sentinels.
Upward the calm of infinite silence deepens,
The sea that flows between high heaven and
    earth,
Musing by whose smooth brink we sometimes
    find
A stray leaf floated from those happier shores,
And hope, perchance not vainly, that some
    flower,

Which we had watered with our holiest tears,
Pale blooms, and yet our scanty garden's best,
O'er the same ocean piloted by love,
May find a haven at the feet of God,
And be not wholly worthless in his sight.

O, high dependence on a higher Power,
Sole stay for all these restless faculties
That wander, Ishmael-like, the desert bare
Wherein our human knowledge hath its home,
Shifting their light-framed tents from day to
    day,
With each new-found oasis, wearied soon,
And only certain of uncertainty!
O, mighty humbleness that feels with awe,
Yet with a vast exulting feels, no less,
That this huge Minster of the Universe,
Whose smallest oratories are glorious worlds,
With painted oriels of dawn and sunset;
Whose carved ornaments are systems grand,
Orion kneeling in his starry niche,
The Lyre whose strings give music audible
To holy ears, and countless splendors more,
Crowned by the blazing Cross high-hung o'er
    all;
Whose organ music is the solemn stops
Of endless Change breathed through by endless
    Good;
Whose choristers are all the morning stars;
Whose altar is the sacred human heart
Whereon Love's candles burn unquenchably,
Trimmed day and night by gentle-handed
    Peace;

With all its arches and its pinnacles
That stretch forever and forever up,
Is founded on the silent heart of God,
Silent, yet pulsing forth exhaustless life
Through the least veins of all created things.

Fit musings these for the departing year;
And God be thanked for such a crystal night
As fills the spirit with good store of thoughts,
That, like a cheering fire of walnut, crackle
Upon the hearthstone of the heart, and cast
A mild home-glow o'er all Humanity!
Yes, though the poisoned shafts of evil doubts
Assail the skyey panoply of Faith,
Though the great hopes which we have had
      for man,
Foes in disguise, because they based belief
On man's endeavor, not on God's decree—
Though these proud-visaged hopes, once turned
      to fly,
Hurl backward many a deadly Parthian dart
That rankles in the soul and makes it sick
With vain regret, nigh verging on despair—
Yet, in such calm and earnest hours as this,
We well can feel how every living heart
That sleeps to-night in palace or in cot,
Or unroofed hovel, or which need hath known
Of other homestead than the arching sky,
Is circled watchfully with seraph fires;
How our own erring will it is that hangs
The flaming sword o'er Eden's unclosed gate.
Which gives free entrance to the pure in heart,
And with its guarding walls doth fence the
      meek.

Sleep then, O Earth, in thy blue-vaulted cradle,
Bent over always by thy mother Heaven!
We all are tall enough to reach God's hand,
And angels are no taller; looking back
Upon the smooth wake of a year o'erpast,
We see the black clouds furling, one by one,
From the advancing majesty of Truth,
And something won for Freedom, whose least
          gain
Is as a firm and rock-built citadel
Wherefrom to launch fresh battle on her foes;
Or, leaning from the time's extremest prow,
If we gaze forward through the blending spray,
And dimly see how much of ill remains,
How many fetters to be sawn asunder
By the slow toil of individual zeal,
Or haply rusted by salt tears in twain,
We feel, with something of a sadder heart,
Yet bracing up our bruised mail the while,
And fronting the old foe with fresher spirit,
How great it is to breathe with human breath,
To be but poor foot-soldiers in the ranks
Of our old exiled king, Humanity;
Encamping after every hard-won field
Nearer and nearer Heaven's happy plains.

Many great souls have gone to rest, and sleep
Under this armor, free and full of peace:
If these have left the earth, yet Truth remains,
Endurance, too, the crowning faculty
Of noble minds, and Love, invincible
By any weapons; and these hem us round
With silence such that all the groaning clank

Of this mad engine men have made of earth
Dulls not some ears for catching purer tones,
That wander from the dim surrounding vast,
Or far more clear melodious prophecies,
The natural music of the heart of man,
Which by kind Sorrow's ministry hath learned
That the true sceptre of all power is love
And humbleness the palace-gate of truth.
What man with soul so blind as sees not here
The first faint tremble of Hope's morning-
    star,
Foretelling how the God-forged shafts of
    dawn,
Fitted already on their golden string,
Shall soon leap earthward with exulting flight
To thrid the dark heart of that evil faith
Whose trust is in the clumsy arms of Force,
The ozier hauberk of a ruder age?
Freedom! thou other name for happy Truth,
Thou warrior-maid, whose steel-clad feet were
    never
Out of the stirrup, nor thy lance uncouched,
Nor thy fierce eye enticed from its watch,
Thou hast learned now, by hero-blood in vain
Poured to enrich the soil which tyrants reap;
By wasted lives of prophets, and of those
Who, by the promise in their souls upheld,
Into the red arms of a fiery death
Went blithely as the golden-girdled bee
Sinks in the sleepy poppy's cup of flame;
By the long woes of nations set at war,
That so the swollen torrent of their wrath
May find a vent, else sweeping off like straws

The thousand cobweb threads, grown cable-
    huge
By time's long gathered dust, but cobwebs
    still,
Which bind the Many that the Few may gain
Leisure to wither by the drought of ease
What heavenly germs in their own souls were
    sown ;—
By all these searching lessons thou hast
    learned
To throw aside thy blood-stained helm and
    spear
And with thy bare brow daunt the enemy's
    front,
Knowing that God will make the lily stalk,
In the soft grasp of naked Gentleness,
Stronger than iron spear to shatter through
The sevenfold toughness of Wrong's idle shield.

A MYSTICAL BALLAD.

I.

THE sunset scarce had dimmed away
Into the twilight's doubtful gray ;
One long cloud o'er the horizon lay,
'Neath which, a streak of bluish white,
Wavered between the day and night ;
Over the pine trees on the hill
The trembly evening-star did thrill
And the new moon, with slender rim,
Through the elm arches gleaming dim,
Filled memory's chalice to the brim.

II.

On such an eve the heart doth grow
Full of surmise, and scarce can know
If it be now or long ago,
Or if indeed it doth exist;—
A wonderful enchanted mist
From the new moon doth wander out,
Wrapping all things in mystic doubt,
So that this world doth seem untrue,
And all our fancies to take hue
From some life ages since gone through.

III.

The maiden sat and heard the flow
Of the west wind so soft and low
The leaves scarce quivered to and fro;
Unbound, her heavy golden hair
Rippled across her bosom bare,
Which gleamed with thrilling snowy white
Far through the magical moonlight:
The breeze rose with a rustling swell,
And from afar there came the smell
Of a long-forgotten lily-bell.

IV.

The dim moon rested on the hill,
But silent, without thought or will,
Where sat the dreamy maiden still;
And now the moon's tip, like a star,
Drew down below the horizon's bar;
To her black noon the night hath grown,
Yet still the maiden sits alone,

Pale as a corpse beneath a stream
And her white bosom still doth gleam
Through the deep midnight like a dream.

v.

Cloudless the morning came and fair,
And lavishly the sun doth share
His gold among her golden hair,
Kindling it all, till slowly so
A glory round her head doth glow;
A withered flower is in her hand,
That grew in some far distant land,
And, silently transfiguréd,
With wide calm eyes, and undrooped head,
They found the stranger-maiden dead.

vi.

A youth, that morn, 'neath other skies,
Felt sudden tears burn in his eyes,
And his heart throng with memories;
All things without him seemed to win
Strange brotherhood with things within,
And he forever felt that he
Walked in the midst of mystery,
And thenceforth, why, he could not tell,
His heart would curdle at the smell
Of his once-cherished lily-bell.

vii.

Something from him had passed away;
Some shifting trembles of clear day,
Through starry crannies in his clay,

Grew bright and steadfast, more and more,
Where all had been dull earth before;
And, through these chinks, like him of old,
His spirit converse high did hold
With clearer loves and wider powers,
That brought him dewy fruits and flowers
From far Elysian groves and bowers.

VIII.

Just on the farther bound of sense,
Unproved by outward evidence,
But known by a deep influence
Which through our grosser clay doth shine
With light unwaning and divine,
Beyond where highest thought can fly
Stretcheth the world of Mystery—
And they not greatly overween
Who deem that nothing true hath been
Save the unspeakable Unseen.

IX.

One step beyond life's work-day things,
One more beat of the soul's broad wings,
One deeper sorrow sometimes brings
The spirit into that great Vast
Where neither future is nor past;
None knoweth how he entered there,
But, waking, finds his spirit where
He thought an angel could not soar,
And, what he called false dreams before,
The very air about his door.

x.

These outward seemings are but shows
Whereby the body sees and knows;
Far down beneath, forever flows
A stream of subtlest sympathies
That make our spirits strangely wise
In awe, and fearful bodings dim
Which, from the sense's outer rim,
Stretch forth beyond our thought and sight,
Fine arteries of circling light,
Pulsed outward from the Infinite.

OPENING POEM TO

A YEAR'S LIFE.

Hope first the youthful Poet leads,
And he is glad to follow her;
Kind is she, and to all his needs
With a free hand doth minister.

But, when sweet Hope at last hath fled,
Cometh her sister, Memory;
She wreaths Hope's garlands round her head,
And strives to seem as fair as she.

Then Hope comes back, and by the hand
She leads a child most fair to see,
Who with a joyous face doth stand
Uniting Aope and Memory.

So brighter grew the Earth around,
And bluer grew the sky above ;
The Poet now his guide hath found,
And follows in the steps of Love.

DEDICATION

TO VOLUME OF POEMS ENTITLED

A YEAR'S LIFE.

THE gentle Una I have loved,
The snowy maiden, pure and mild
Since ever by her side I roved,
Through ventures strange, a wondering child,
In fantasy a Red Cross Knight,
Burning for her dear sake to fight.

If there be one who can, like her,
Make sunshine in life's shady places,
One in whose holy bosom stir
As many gentle household graces—
And such I think there needs must be—
Will she accept this book from me?

THRENODIA.

Gone, gone from us! and shall we see
Those sybil-leaves of destiny,
Those calm eyes, nevermore?
Those deep, dark eyes so warm and bright,
Wherein the fortunes of the man
Lay slumbering in prophetic light,
In characters a child might scan?
So bright, and gone forth utterly?
O stern word—Nevermore!

The stars of those two gentle eyes
Will shine no more on earth;
Quenched are the hopes that had their birth,
As we watched them slowly rise,
Stars of a mother's fate;
And she would read them o'er and o'er,
Pondering, as she sate,
Over their dear astrology,
Which she had conned and conned before,
Deeming she needs must read aright
What was writ so passing bright.
And yet, alas! she knew not why,
Her voice would falter in its song,
And tears would slide from out her eye,
Silent, as they were doing wrong.
Her heart was like a wind-flower, bent
Even to breaking with the balmy dew,

Turning its heavenly nourishment
(That filled with tears its eyes of blue,
Like a sweet suppliant that weeps in prayer,
Making her innocency show more fair,
Albeit unwitting of the ornament,)
Into a load too great for it to bear:
O stern word—Nevermore!

The tongue, that scarce had learned to claim
An entrance to a mother's heart
By that dear talisman, a mother's name,
Sleeps all forgetful of its art!
I loved to see the infant soul
(How mighty in the weakness
Of its untutored meekness!)
Peep timidly from out its nest,
His lips, the while,
Fluttering with half-fledged words,
Or hushing to a smile
That more than words expressed,
When his glad mother on him stole
And snatched him to her breast!
O, thoughts were brooding in those eyes,
That would have soared like strong-winged
      birds
Far, far into the skies,
Gladdening the earth with song
And gushing harmonies,
Had he but tarried with us long!
O stern word—Nevermore!

How peacefully they rest,
Crossfolded there

Upon his little breast,
Those small, white hands that ne'er were still
    before,
But ever sported with his mother's hair,
Or the plain cross that on her breast she wore!
Her heart no more will beat
To feel the touch of that soft palm,
That ever seemed a new surprise
Sending glad thoughts up to her eyes
To bless him with their holy calm—
Sweet thoughts! they made her eyes as
    sweet.
How quiet are the hands
That wove those pleasant bands!
But that they do not rise and sink
With his calm breathing, I should think
That he were dropped asleep;
Alas! too deep, too deep
Is this his slumber!
Time scarce can number
The years ere he will wake again—
O, may we see his eyelids open then!
O stern word—Nevermore!

    As the airy gossamere,
Floating in the sunlight clear,
Where'er it toucheth clinging tightly
Round glossy leaf or stump unsightly,
So from his spirit wandered out
Tendrils spreading all about,
Knitting all things to its thrall
With a perfect love of all:
O stern word—Nevermore!
    9

He did but float a little way
Adown the stream of time,
With dreamy eyes watching the ripples play,
Or listening to their fairy chime ;
His slender sail
Ne'er felt the gale;
He did but float a little way,
And, putting to the shore
While yet 't was early day,
Went calmly on his way,
To dwell with us no more !
No jarring did he feel,
No grating on his vessel's keel ;
A strip of silver sand
Mingled the waters with the land
Where he was seen no more :
O stern word—Nevermore!

Full short his journey was ; no dust
Of earth unto his sandals clave ;
The weary weight that old men must,
He bore not to the grave.
He seemed a cherub who had lost his way
And wandered hither, so his stay
With us was short, and 't was most meet
That he should be no delver in Earth's clod,
Nor need to pause and cleanse his feet
To stand before his God ;
O blest word—Evermore!

THE SERENADE.

GENTLE, Lady, be thy sleeping,
Peaceful may thy dreamings be,
While around thy soul is sweeping,
Dreamy-winged, our melody;
Chant we, Brothers, sad and slow,
Let our song be soft and low
As the voice of other years,
Let our hearts within us melt,
To gentleness, as if we felt
The dropping of our mother's tears.

Lady! now our song is bringing
Back again thy childhood's hours—
Hearest thou the humbee singing
Drowsily among the flowers?
Sleepily, sleepily
In the noontide swayeth he,
Half rested on the slender stalks
That edge those well-known garden **walks;**
Hearest thou the fitful whirring
Of the humbird's viewless wings—
Feel'st not round thy heart the stirring
Of childhood's half-forgotten things?

Seest thou the dear old dwelling
With the woodbine round the door?
Brothers, soft! her breast is swelling

With the busy thoughts of yore;
Lowly sing ye, sing ye mildly,
Rouse her spirit not so wildly,
Lest she sleep not any more.
'Tis the pleasant summertide,
Open stands the window wide—
Whose voices, Lady, art thou drinking?
Who sings that best beloved tune
In a clear note, rising, sinking,
Like a thrush's song in June?
Whose laugh is that which rings so clear
And joyous in thine eager ear?

Lower, Brothers, yet more low
Weave the song in mazy twines;
She heareth now the west wind blow
At evening through the clump of pines;
O! mournful is their tone,
As of a crazèd thing
Who, to herself alone,
Is ever murmuring,
Through the night and through the day,
For something that hath past away.
Often, Lady, hast thou listened,
Often have thy blue eyes glistened,
When the summer evening breeze
Moaned sadly through those lonely trees,
Or with the fierce wind from the north
Wrung their mournful music forth.
Ever the river floweth
In an unbroken stream,
Ever the west wind bloweth,
Murmuring as he goeth,

And mingling with her dream:
Onward still the river sweepeth
With a sound of long-agone;
Lowly, Brothers, lo! she weepeth,
She is now no more alone;
Long-loved forms and long-loved faces
Round about her pillow throng,
Through her memory's desert places
Flow the waters of our song.
Lady! if thy life be holy
As when thou wert yet a child,
Though our song be melancholy,
It will stir no anguish wild;
For the soul that hath lived well,
For the soul that child-like is,
There is quiet in the spell
That brings back early memories.

SONG.

I.

LIFT up the curtains of thine eyes
    And let their light out-shine!
Let me adore the mysteries
    Of those mild orbs of thine,
Which ever queenly calm do roll,
Attunèd to an ordered soul!

II.

Open thy lips yet once again
    And, while my soul doth hush

With awe, pour forth that holy strain
  Which seemeth me to gush,
A fount of music, running o'er
From thy deep spirit's inmost core!

II

The melody that dwells in thee
  Begets in me as well
A spiritual harmony,
  A mild and blessed spell;
Far, far above earth's atmosphere
  rise, whene'er thy voice I hear.

THE DEPARTED.

Not they alone are the departed,
Who have laid them down to sleep
In the grave narrow and lonely,
Not for them only do I vigils keep,
Not for them only am I heavy-hearted,
Not for them only!

Many, many, there are many
Who no more are with me here,
As cherished, as beloved as any
Whom I have seen upon the bier.
I weep to think of those old faces,
To see them in their grief of mirth;
I weep—for there are empty places
Around my heart's once crowded hearth;
The cold ground doth not cover them,
The grass hath not grown over them,

Yet are they gone from me on earth ;—
O ! how more bitter is this weeping,
Than for those lost ones who are sleeping
Where sun will shine and flowers blow,
Where gentle winds will whisper low,
And the stars have them in their keeping!
Wherefore from me who loved you so
O ! wherefore did ye go ?
I have shed full many a tear,
I have wrestled oft in prayer—
But ye do not come again;
How could anything so dear,
How could anything so fair,
Vanish like the summer rain?
No, no, it cannot be,
But ye are still with me !

    And yet, O ! where art thou,
Childhood, with sunny brow
And floating hair ?
Where art thou hiding now?
I have sought thee everywhere,
All among the shrubs and flowers
Of those garden-walks of ours—
Thou art not there !
When the shadow of Night's wings
Hath darkened all the Earth,
I listen for thy gambolings
Beside the cheerful hearth—
Thou art not there !
I listen to the far-off bell,
I murmur o'er the little songs
Which thou didst love so well,

Pleasant memories come in throngs
And mine eyes are blurred with tears,
But no glimpse of thee appears :
Lonely am I in the Winter, lonely in the
      Spring,
Summer and Harvest bring no trace of thee—
Oh! whither, whither art thou wandering,
Thou who didst once so cleave to me?

    And Love is gone;—
I have seen him come,
I have seen him, too, depart,
Leaving desolate his home,
His bright home in my heart.
I am alone!
Cold, cold is his hearth-stone,
Wide open stands the door ;
The frolic and the gentle one
Shall I see no more, no more?
At the fount the bowl is broken,
I shall drink it not again,
All my longing prayers are spoken,
And felt, ah, woe is me, in vain!
Oh, childish hopes and childish fancies,
Whither have ye fled away ?
I long for you in mournful trances,
I long for you by night and day ;
Beautiful thoughts that once were mine,
Might I but win you back once more,
Might ye about my being twine
And cluster as ye did of yore !
O! do not let me pray in vain—
How good and happy I should be,

How free from every shade of pain,
If ye would come again to me!
O, come again! come, come again!
Hath the sun forgot its brightness,
Have the stars forgot to shine,
That they bring not their wonted lightness
To this weary heart of mine?
'Tis not the sun that shone on thee,
Happy childhood, long ago—
Not the same stars silently
Looking on the same bright snow—
Not the same that Love and I
Together watched in days gone by!
No, not the same, alas for me!

Would God that those who early went
To the house dark and low,
For whom our mourning heads were bent,
For whom our steps were slow;
O, would that these alone had left us,
That Fate of these alone had reft us,
Would God indeed that it were so!
Many leaves too soon must wither,
Many flowers too soon must die,
Many bright ones wandering hither,
We know not whence, we know not why,
Like the leaves and like the flowers,
Vanish, ere the summer hours,
That brought them to us, have gone by.

O for the hopes and for the feelings,
Childhood, that I shared with thee—
The high resolves, the bright revealings

Of the soul's might, which thou gav'st me,
Gentle Love, woe worth the day,
Woe worth the hour when thou wert born,
Woe worth the day thou fled'st away—
A shade across the wind-waved corn—
A dewdrop falling from the leaves
Chance-shaken in a summer's morn!
Woe, woe is me! my sick heart grieves,
Companionless and anguish-worn!
I know it well, our manly years
Must be baptized in bitter tears;
Full many fountains must run dry
That youth has dreamed for long hours by,
Choked by convention's siroc blast
Or drifting sands of many cares;
Slowly they leave us all at last,
And cease their flowing unawares.

THE BOBOLINK.

Anacreon of the meadow,
Drunk with the joy of spring!
Beneath the tall pine's voiceful shadow
I lie and drink thy jargoning;
My soul is full with melodies,
One drop would overflow it,
And send the tears into mine eyes—
But what car'st thou to know it?
Thy heart is free as mountain air,
And of thy lays thou hast no care,
Scattering them gaily everywhere,
Happy, unconscious poet!

Upon a tuft of meadow grass,
While thy loved-one tends the nest,
Thou swayest as the breezes pass,
Unburthening thine o'erfull breast
Of the crowded songs that fill it,
Just as joy may choose to will it.
Lord of thy love and liberty,
The blithest bird of merry May,
Thou turnest thy bright eyes on me,
That say as plain as eye can say—
"Here sit we, here in the summer weather,
I and my modest mate together;
Whatever your wise thoughts may be,
Under that gloomy old pine tree,
We do not value them a feather."

Now, leaving earth and me behind,
Thou beatest up against the wind,
Or, floating slowly down before it,
Above thy grass-hid nest thou flutterest
And thy bridal love-song utterest,
Raining showers of music o'er it,
Weary never, still thou trillest,
Spring-gladsome lays,
As of moss-rimmed water-brooks
Murmuring through pebbly nooks
In quiet summer days.
My heart with happiness thou fillest,
I seem again to be a boy
Watching thee, gay, blithesome lover,
O'er the bending grass-tops hover,
Quivering thy wings for joy.
There 's something in the apple blossom,

The greening grass and bobolink's song,
That wakes again within my bosom
Feelings which have slumbered long.
As long, long years ago I wandered,
I seem to wander even yet,
The hours the idle school-boy squandered,
The man would die ere he 'd forget.
O hours that frosty eld deemed wasted,
Nodding his gray head toward my books,
I dearer prize the lore I tasted
With you, among the trees and brooks,
Than all that I have gained since then
From learned books or study-withered men!
Nature, thy soul was one with mine,
And, as a sister by a younger brother
Is loved, each flowing to the other,
Such love from me was thine.
Or wert thou not more like a loving mother
With sympathy and loving power to heal,
Against whose heart my throbbing heart I 'd
    lay
And moan my childish sorrows all away,
Till calm and holiness would o'er me steal?
Was not the golden sunset a dear friend?
Found I no kindness in the silent moon,
And the green trees, whose tops did sway and
    bend,
Low singing evermore their pleasant tune?
Felt I no heart in dim and solemn woods—
No loved-one's voice in lonely solitudes?
Yes, yes! unhoodwinked then my spirit's
    eyes,
Blind leaders had not *taught me* to be wise.

Dear hours! which now again I over-live,
Hearing and seeing with ears and eyes
Of childhood, ye were bees, that to the hive
Of my young heart came laden with rich prize,
Gathered in fields and woods and sunny dells,
    to be
My spirit's food in days more wintery
Yea, yet again ye come! ye come!
And, like a child once more at home
After long sojourning in alien climes,
I lie upon my mother's breast,
Feeling the blessedness of rest,
And dwelling in the light of other times

O ye whose living is not *Life,*
Whose dying is but death,
Song, empty toil and petty strife,
Rounded with loss of breath!
Go, look on Nature's countenance,
Drink in the blessing of her glance;
Look on the sunset, hear the wind,
The cataract, the awful thunder;
Go, worship by the sea;
Then, and then only, shall ye find,
With ever-growing wonder,
Man is not all in all to ye;
Go with a meek and humble soul,
Then shall the scales of self unroll
From off your eyes—the weary packs
Drop from your heavy-laden backs;
And ye shall see,
With reverent and hopeful eyes,
Glowing with new-born energies,
How great a thing it is to BE!

FORGETFULNESS.

THERE's a haven of sure rest
  From the loud world's bewildering stress:
As a bird dreaming on her nest,
As dew hid in a rose's breast,
As Hesper in the glowing West;
    So the heart sleeps
    In thy calm deeps,
  Serene Forgetfulness!

No sorrow in that place may be,
  The noise of life grows less and less:
As moss far down within the sea,
As, in white lily caves, a bee,
As life in a hazy reverie;
    So the heart's wave
    In thy dim cave,
  Hushes, Forgetfulness!

Duty and care fade far away,
  What toil may be we cannot guess:
As a ship anchored in the bay,
As a cloud at summer-noon astray,
As water-blooms in a breezeless day;
    So, 'neath thine eyes,
    The full heart lies,
  And dreams, Forgetfulness!

SONG.

I.

What reck I of the stars, when I
  May gaze into thine eyes,
O'er which the brown hair flowingly
  Is parted maidenwise
From thy pale forehead, calm and bright,
Over thy cheeks so rosy white?

II.

What care I for the red moon-rise?
  Far liefer would I sit
And watch the joy within thine eyes
  Gush up at sight of it;
Thyself my queenly moon shall be,
Ruling my heart's deep tides for me!

III.

What heed I if the sky be blue?
  So are thy holy eyes,
And bright with shadows ever new
  Of changeful sympathies,
Which in thy soul's unruffled deep
Rest evermore, but never sleep.

THE POET.

He who hath felt Life's mystery
  Press on him like thick night,
Whose soul hath known no history
  But struggling after light;—
He who hath seen dim shapes arise
  In the soundless depths of soul,
Which gaze on him with meaning eyes
  Full of the mighty whole,
Yet will no word of healing speak,
  Although he pray night-long,
"O, help me, save me! I am weak,
  And ye are wondrous strong!"—
Who, in the midnight dark and deep,
  Hath felt a voice of might
Come echoing through the halls of sleep
  From the lone heart of Night,
And, starting from his restless bed,
  Hath watched and wept to know
What meant that oracle of dread
  That stirred his being so;
He who hath felt how strong and great
  This Godlike soul of man,
And looked full in the eyes of Fate,
  Since Life and Thought began;
The armor of whose moveless trust
  Knoweth no spot of weakness,

Who hath trod fear into the dust
  Beneath the feet of meekness;—
He who hath calmly borne his cross,
  Knowing himself the king
Of time, nor counted it a loss
  To learn by suffering;—
And who hath worshipped woman still
  With a pure soul and lowly,
Nor ever hath in deed or will
  Profaned her temple holy—
He is the Poet, him unto
  The gift of song is given, .
Whose life is lofty, strong, and true,
  Who never fell from Heaven;
He is the Poet, from his lips
  To live forevermore,
Majestical as full-sailed ships,
  The words of Wisdom pour.

FLOWERS.

"Hail be thou, holie hearbe,
  Growing on the ground,
All in the mount Calvary
  First wert thou found;
Thou art good for manie a sore,
  Thou healest manie a wound,
In the name of sweete Jesus
  I take thee from the ground."
            —*Ancient Charm-verse.*

I.

When, from a pleasant ramble, home
Fresh-stored with quiet thoughts, I come,
I pluck some wayside flower
And press it in the choicest nook
Of a much-loved and oft-read book;
And, when upon its leaves I look
In a less happy hour,
Dear memory bears me far away
Unto her fairy bower,
And on her breast my head I lay,
While, in a motherly, sweet strain,
She sings me gently back again
To by-gone feelings, until they
Seem children born of yesterday.

II.

Yes, many a story of past hours
I read in these dear withered flowers
And once again I seem to be
Lying beneath the old oak tree,
And looking up into the sky,
Through thick leaves rifted fitfully,
Lulled by the rustling of the vine,
Or the faint low of far-off kine;
And once again I seem
To watch the whirling bubbles flee,
Through shade and gleam alternately,
Down the vine-bowered stream;
Or 'neath the odorous linden trees,
When summer twilight lingers long,
To hear the flowing of the breeze

And unseen insects' slumberous song,
That mingle into one and seem
Like dim murmurs of a dream;
Fair faces, too, I seem to see,
Smiling from pleasant eyes at me,
And voices sweet I hear,
That, like remembered melody,
Flow through my spirit's ear.

III.

A poem every flower is,
And every leaf a line,
And with delicious memories
They fill this heart of mine :
No living blossoms are so clear.
As these dead relics treasured here;
One tells of love, of friendship one,
Love's quiet after-sunset time,
When the all-dazzling light is gone,
And, with the soul's low vesper-chime,
O'er half its heaven doth out-flow
A holy calm and steady glow.
Some are gay feast-song, some are dirges,
In some a joy with sorrow merges ;
One sings the shadowed woods, and one the roar
Of ocean's everlasting surges,
Tumbling upon the beach's hard-beat floor,
Or sliding backward from the shore
To meet the landward waves and slowly plunge
        once more.
O flowers of grace, I bless ye all
By the dear faces ye recall !

IV.

Upon the banks of Life's deep streams
Full many a flower groweth,
Which with a wondrous fragrance teems,
And in the silent water gleams,
And trembles as the water floweth,
Many a one the wave upteareth,
Washing ever the roots away,
And far upon its bosom beareth,
To bloom no more in Youth's glad May;
As farther on the river runs,
Flowing more deep and strong,
Only a few pale, scattered ones
Are seen the dreary banks along;
And where those flowers do not grow,
The river floweth dark and chill,
Its voice is sad, and with its flow
Mingles ever a sense of ill;
Then, Poet, thou who gather dost
Of Life's best flowers the brightest,
O, take good heed they be not lost
While with the angry flood thou fightest!

V.

In the cool grottoes of the soul,
Whence flows thought's crystal river,
Whence songs of joy forever roll
To Him who is the Giver—
There store thou them, where fresh and
    green
Their leaves and blossoms may be seen,
A spring of joy that faileth never;

There store thou them, and they shall be
A blessing and a peace to thee,
And in their youth and purity
Thou shalt be young forever!
Then, with their fragrance rich and rare,
Thy living shall be rife,
Strength shall be thine thy cross to bear,
And they shall be a chaplet fair,
Breathing a pure and holy air,
To crown thy holy life.

VI.

    O Poet! above all men blest,
Take heed that thus thou store them;
Love, Hope, and Faith shall ever rest,
Sweet birds (upon how sweet a nest!)
Watchfully brooding o'er them.
And from those flowers of Paradise
Scatter thou many a blessed seed,
Wherefrom an offspring may arise
To cheer the hearts and light the eyes
Of after-voyagers in their need.
They shall not fall on stony ground,
But, yielding all their hundred-fold,
Shall shed a peacefulness around,
Whose strengthening joy may not be told,
So shall thy name be blest of all,
And thy remembrance never die;
For of that seed shall surely fall
In the fair garden of Eternity.
Exult then in the nobleness
Of this thy work so holy,
Yet be not thou one jot the less

Humble and meek and lowly,
But let thine exultation be
The reverence of a bended knee,
And by thy life a poem write,
Built strongly day by day—
And on the rock of Truth and Right
Its deep foundations lay

VII.

It is thy DUTY!   Guaru it well!
For unto thee hath much been given,
And thou canst make this life a Hell,
Or Jacob's-ladder up to Heaven.
Let not thy baptism in Life's wave
Make thee like him whom Homer sings—
A sleeper in a living grave,
Callous and hard to outward things;
But open all thy soul and sense
To every blessèd influence
That from the heart of Nature springs:
Then shall thy Life-flowers be to thee,
When thy best years are told,
As much as these have been to me—
Yea, more, a thousand-fold!

THE LOVER.

I.

Go ROAM the world from East to West,
Search every land beneath the sky,
You cannot find a man so blest,
A king so powerful as I,
Though you should seek eternally.

II.

For I a gentle lover be,
Sitting at my loved-one's side;
She giveth her whole soul to me
Without a wish or thought of pride,
And she shall be my cherished bride.

III.

No show of gaudiness hath she,
She doth not flash with jewels rare;
In beautiful simplicity
She weareth leafy garlands fair,
Or modest flowers in her hair.

IV.

Sometimes she dons a robe of green,
Sometimes a robe of snowy white,
But, in whatever garb she 's seen,
It seems most beautiful and right,
And is the loveliest to my sight.

V.

Not I her lover am alone,
Yet unto all she doth suffice,
None jealous is, and every one
Reads love and truth within her eyes,
And deemeth her his own dear prize.

VI.

And so thou art, Eternal Nature!
Yes, bride of Heaven, so thou art;
Thou wholly lovest every creature,
Giving to each no stinted part,
But filling every peaceful heart.

TO E. W. G.

"Dear Child! dear happy Girl! if thou appear
Heedless—untouched with awe or serious
    thought,
Thy nature is not therefore less divine:
Thou liest in Abraham's bosom all the year;
And worship'st at the Temple's inner shrine,
God being with thee when we know it not."
                              — *Wordsworth.*

As through a strip of sunny light
A white dove flashes swiftly on,
So suddenly before my sight
Thou gleamed'st a moment and wert gone;
And yet I long shall bear in mind
The pleasant thoughts thou left'st behind.

Thou mad'st me happy with thine eyes,
And happy with thine open smile,
And, as I write, sweet memories
Come thronging round me all the while;
Thou mad'st me happy with thine eyes—
And gentle feelings long forgot
Looked up and oped their eyes,
Like violets when they see a spot
Of summer in the skies.

Around thy playful lips did glitter
Heat-lightnings of a girlish scorn;
Harmless they were, for nothing bitter
In thy dear heart was ever born—
That merry heart that could not lie
Within its warm nest quietly,
But ever from each full, dark eye
Was looking kindly night and morn.

There was an archness in thine eyes,
Born of the gentlest mockeries,
And thy light laughter rang as clear
As water-drops I loved to hear
In days of boyhood, as they fell
Tinkling far down the dim, still well;
And with its sound come back once more
The feelings of my early years,
And half aloud I murmured o'er—
"Sure I have heard that sound before,
It is so pleasant in mine ears."

Whenever thou didst look on me
I thought of merry birds,

And something of spring's melody
Came to me in thy words ;
Thy thoughts did dance and bound along
Like happy children in their play,
Whose hearts run over into song
For gladness of the summer's day ;
And mine grew dizzy with the sight,
Still feeling lighter and more light,
Till, joining hands, they whirled away,
As blithe and merrily as they.

I bound a larch-twig round with flowers,
Which thou didst twine among thy hair,
And gladsome were the few, short hours
When I was with thee there ;
So now that thou art far away,
Safe-nestled in thy warmer clime,
In memory of a happier day
I twine this simple wreath of rhyme.

Dost mind how she, whom thou dost love
More than in light words may be said,
A coronal of amaranth wove
About thy duly-sobered head,
Which kept itself a moment still
That she might have her gentle will?
Thy childlike grace and purity
O keep forevermore,
And as thou art, still strive to be,
That on the farther shore
Of Time's dark waters ye may meet,
And she may twine around thy brow
A wreath of those bright flowers that grow
Where blessed angels set their feet!

ISABEL.

As THE leaf upon the tree,
Fluttering, gleaming constantly,
Such a lightsome thing was she,
My gay and gentle Isabel!
Her heart was fed with love-springs sweet,
And in her face you 'd see it beat
To hear the sound of welcome feet—
And were not mine so, Isabel?

She knew it not, but she was fair,
And like a moonbeam was her hair,
That falls where flowing ripples are
In summer evenings, Isabel!
Her heart and tongue were scarce apart,
Unwittingly her lips would part,
And love came gushing from her heart,
The woman's heart of Isabel.

So pure her flesh-garb, and like dew,
That in her features glimmered through
Each working of her spirit true,
In wondrous beauty, Isabel!
A sunbeam struggling through thick leaves,
A reaper's song 'mid yellow sheaves,
Less gladsome were;—my spirit grieves
To think of thee, mild Isabel!

I know not when I loved the first;
Not loving, I had been accurst,
Yet, having loved, my heart will burst,
Longing for thee, dear Isabel!
With silent tears my cheeks are wet,
I would be calm, I would forget,
But thy blue eyes gaze on me yet,
When stars have risen, Isabel.

The winds mourn for thee, Isabel,
The flowers expect thee in the dell,
Thy gentle spirit loved them well,
And I for thy sake, Isabel!
The sunsets seem less lovely now
Than when, leaf checkered, on thy brow
They fell as lovingly as thou
Lingered'st till moon-rise, Isabel!

At dead of night I seem to see
Thy fair, pale features constantly
Upturned in silent prayer for me,
O'er moveless clasped hands, Isabel!
I call thee, thou dost not reply;
The stars gleam coldly on thine eye,
As like a dream thou flittest by,
And leav'st me weeping, Isabel!

MUSIC.

I.

I seem to lie with drooping eyes,
  Dreaming sweet dreams,
Half longings and half memories,
  In woods where streams
With trembling shades and whirling gleams,
  Many and bright,
  In song and light,
  Are ever, ever flowing;
While the wind, if we list to the rustling grass,
Which numbers his footsteps as they pass,
  Seems scarcely to be blowing;
And the far-heard voice of Spring,
From sunny slopes comes wandering,
Calling the violets from the sleep,
That bound them under the snow-drifts deep,
To open their childlike, asking eyes
On the new summer's paradise,
And mingled with the gurgling waters—
  As the dreamy witchery
Of Achelous' silver-voiced daughters
  Rose and fell with the heaving sea,
Whose great heart swelled with ecstasy—
The song of many a floating bird,
  Winding through the rifted trees,
Is dreamily half-heard—
  A sister stream of melodies

Rippled by the flutterings
Of rapture-quivered wings.

II.

And now beside a cataract
I lie, and through my soul,
From over me and under,
The never-ceasing thunder
Arousingly doth roll;
Through the darkness all compact,
Through the trackless sea of gloom,
Sad and deep I hear it boom;
At intervals the cloud is cracked
And a livid flesh doth hiss
   Downward from its floating home,
Lighting up the precipice
   And the never-resting foam
With a dim and ghastly glare,
Which, for a heart-beat, in the air,
   Shows the sweeping shrouds
   Of the midnight clouds
And their wildly-scattered hair.

III.

Now listening to a woman's tone,
In a wood I sit alone—
Alone because our souls are one;—
All around my heart it flows,
Lulling me in deep repose;
I fear to speak, I fear to move,
Lest I should break the spell I love—
Low and gentle, calm and clear,
Into my inmost soul it goes,

As if my brother dear,
Who is no longer here,
Had bended from the sky
And murmured in my ear
A strain of that high harmony,
Which they may sing alone
Who worship round the throne.

IV.

Now in a fairy boat,
On the bright waves of song,
Full merrily I float,
Merrily float along;
My helm is veered, I care not how,
My white sail bellies over me,
And bright as gold the ripples be
That plash beneath the bow;
Before, behind,
They feel the wind,
And they are dancing joyously—
While, faintly heard, along the far-off shore
The surf goes plunging with a lingering roar;
Or anchored in a shadowy cove,
Entranced with harmonies,
Slowly I sink and rise
As the slow waves of music move.

V.

Now softly dashing,
Bubbling, plashing,
Mazy, dreamy,
Faint and streamy,

Ripples into ripples melt,
Not so strongly heard as felt;
Now rapid and quick,
While the heart beats thick,
The music's silver wavelets crowd,
Distinct and clear, but never loud;
And now all solemnly and slow,
In mild, deep tones they warble low,
Like the glad song of angels, when
They sang good will and peace to men;
Now faintly heard and far,
As if the spirit's ears
Had caught the anthem of a star
  Chanting with his brother-spheres
In the midnight dark and deep,
When the body is asleep
And wondrous shadows pour in streams
From the twofold gate of dreams;
Now onward roll the billows, swelling
With a tempest-sound of might,
As of voices doom foretelling
  To the silent ear of Night;
And now a mingled ecstasy
  Of all sweet sounds it is;—
    O! who may tell the agony
      Of rapture such as this?

VI.

I have drunk of the drink of immortals,
  I have drunk of the life-giving wine,
And now I may pass the bright portals
  That open into a realm divine!

I have drunk it through mine ears
  In the ecstasy of song,
When mine eyes would fill with tears
  That its life were not more long;
I have drunk it through mine eyes
  In beauty's every shape,
And now around my soul it lies,
  No juice of earthly grape!
Wings! wings are given to me,
  I can flutter, I can rise,
Like a new life gushing through me
  Sweep the heavenly harmonies!

SONG.

O! I must look on that sweet face once more
  before I die;
God grant that it may lighten up with joy
  when I draw nigh;
God grant that she may look on me as kindly
  as she seems
In the long night, the restless night, i' the
  sunny land of dreams!

I hoped, I thought, she loved me once, and
  yet, I know not why,
There is a coldness in her speech, and a coldness in her eye.
Something that in another's look would not
  seem cold to me,
And yet like ice I feel it chill the heart of
  memory.

11

She does not come to greet me so frankly as
    she did,
And in her utmost openness I feel there's some-
    thing hid ;
She almost seems to shun me, as if she thought
    that I
Might win her gentle heart again to feelings
    long gone by.

I sought the first spring-buds for her, the
    fairest and the best,
And she wore them for their loveliness upon
    her spotless breast,
The blood-root and the violet, the frail anem-
    one,
She wore them, and alas! I deemed it was for
    love of me!

As flowers in a darksome place stretch forward
    to the light,
So to the memory of her I turn by day and
    night;
As flowers in a darksome place grow thin and
    pale and wan,
So is it with my darkened heart, now that her
    light is gone.

The thousand little things that love doth
    treasure up for aye,
And brood upon with moistened eyes when
    she that's loved's away ;

The word, the look, the smile, the blush, the
    ribbon that she wore,
Each day they grow more dear to me, and pain
    me more and more.

My face I cover with my hands, and bitterly
    I weep,
That the quick-gathering sands of life should
    choke a love so deep,
And that the stream, so pure and bright, must
    turn it from its track,
Or to the heart-springs, whence it rose, roll
    its full waters back!

As calm as doth the lily float close by the
    lakelet's brim,
So calm and spotless, down time's stream, her
    peaceful days did swim,
And I had longed, and dreamed, and prayed,
    that closely by her side,
Down to a haven still and sure, my happy life
    might glide.

But now, alas! those golden days of youth
    and hope are o'er,
And I must dream those dreams of joy, those
    guiltless dreams no more;
Yet there is something in my heart that whis-
    pers ceaselessly,
"Would God that I might see that face once
    more before I die!"

IANTHE.

I.

THERE is a light within her eyes,
Like gleams of wandering fire-flies;
From light to shade it leaps and moves
Whenever in her soul arise
The holy shapes of things she loves;
Fitful it shines and changes ever,
Like star-lit ripples on a river,
Or summer sunshine on the eaves
Of silver-trembling poplar leaves,
Where the lingering dewdrops quiver.
I may not tell the blessedness
Her mild eyes send to mine,
The sunset-tinted haziness
Of their mysterious shine,
The dim and holy mournfulness
Of their mellow light divine;
The shadow of the lashes lie
Over them so lovingly,
That they seem to melt away
In a doubtful twilight-gray,
While I watch the stars arise
In the evening of her eyes.
I love it, yet I almost dread
To think what it foreshadoweth;
And, when I muse how I have read
That such strange light betokened death—

Instead of fire-fly gleams, I see
Wild corpse-lights gliding waveringly.

II.

With wayward thoughts her eyes are
  bright,
Like shiftings of the northern-light,
Hither, thither, swiftly glance they,
In a mazy twining dance they,
Like ripply lights the sunshine weaves,
Thrown backward from a shaken nook,
Below some tumbling water-brook,
On the o'erarching platan-leaves,
All through her glowing face they flit,
And rest in their deep dwelling-place,
Those fathomless blue eyes of hers,
Till, from her burning soul re-lit,
While her upheaving bosom stirs,
They stream again across her face
And with such hope and glory fill it,
Death could not have the heart to chill it.
Yet when their wild light fades again,
I feel a sudden sense of pain,
As if, while yet her eyes were gleaming,
And like a shower of sun-lit rain
Bright fancies from her face were streaming,
Her trembling soul might flit away
As swift and suddenly as they.

III.

A wild, inspired earnestness
  Her inmost being fills,

And eager self-forgetfulness,
   That speaks not what it wills,
But what unto her soul is given,
A living oracle from Heaven,
Which scarcely in her breast is born
When on her trembling lips it thrills,
And, like a burst of golden skies
Through storm-clouds on a sudden torn,
Like a glory of the morn,
Beams marvellously from her eyes.
And then, like a Spring-swollen river,
Roll the deep waves of her full-hearted
      thought
   Crested with sun-lit spray,
   Her wild lips curve and quiver,
And my rapt soul, on the strong tide up-
      caught
   Unwittingly is borne away,
   Lulled by a dreamful music ever,
   Far—through the solemn twilight-gray
Of hoary woods—through valleys green
   Which the trailing vine embowers,
And where the purple-clustered grapes are
      seen
Deep-glowing through rich clumps of waving
      flowers—
   Now over foaming rapids swept
   And with maddening rapture shook—
Now gliding where the water-plants have
      slept
   For ages in a moss rimmed nook—
   Enwoven by a wild-eyed band
      Of earth-forgetting dreams,

I float to a delicious land
By a sunset heaven spanned,
And musical with streams ;—
Around, the calm, majestic forms
And god-like eyes of early Greece I see,
Or listen, till my spirit warms,
To songs of courtly chivalry,
Or weep, unmindful if my tears be seen,
For the meek, suffering love of poor Undine.

IV.

Her thoughts are never memories,
But ever changeful, ever new,
Fresh and beautiful as dew
That in a dell at noontide lies,
Or, at the close of summer day,
The pleasant breath of new-mown hay:
Swiftly they come and pass
As golden birds across the sun,
As light-gleams on tall meadow-grass
Which the wind just breathes upon.
And when she speaks, her eyes I see
Down-gushing through their silken lattices,
Like stars that quiver tremblingly
Through leafy branches of the trees,
And her pale cheeks do flush and glow
With speaking flashes bright and rare
As crimson North-lights on new-fallen snow,
From out the veiling of her hair—
Her careless hair that scatters down
On either side her eyes,
A waterfall leaf-tinged with brown
And lit with the sunrise.

v.

When first I saw her, not of earth,
But heavenly both in grief and mirth,
I thought her; she did seem
As fair and full of mystery,
As bodiless, as forms we see
In the rememberings of a dream;
A moonlit mist, a strange, dim light,
Circled her spirit from my sight;—
Each day more beautiful she grew,
    More earthly, every day,
Yet that mysterious, moony hue
    Faded not all away;
She has a sister's sympathy
With all the wanderers of the sky,
But most I 've seen her bosom stir
    When moonlight round her fell,
For the mild moon it loveth her,
    She loveth it as well,
And of their love perchance this grace
Was born into her wondrous face.
I cannot tell how it may be,
For both, methinks, can scarce be true,
Still, as she earthly grew to me,
She grew more heavenly too;
    She seems one born in Heaven
       With earthly feelings,
    For, while unto her soul are given
       More pure revealings
    Of holiest love and truth,
Yet is the mildness of her eyes
Made up of quickest sympathies,
    Of kindliness and ruth;

So, though some shade of awe doth stir
Our souls for one so far above us,
We feel secure that she will love us,
And cannot keep from loving her.
She is a poem, which to me
In speech and look is written bright,
And to her life's rich harmony
Doth ever sing itself aright;
Dear, glorious creature!
With eyes so dewy bright,
  And tenderest feeling
  Itself revealing
In every look and feature,
Welcome as a homestead light
To one long-wandering in a clouded night;
  O, lovelier for her woman's weakness,
    Which yet is strongly mailed
  In armor of courageous meekness
    And faith that never failed!

VI.

  Early and late, at her soul's gate,
Sits Chastity in warderwise,
No thoughts unchallenged, small or great,
Go thence into her eyes;
Nor may a low, unworthy thought
Beyond that virgin warder win,
Nor one, whose password is not "ought,"
May go without or enter in.
I call her, seeing those pure eyes,
The Eve of a new Paradise,
Which she by gentie word and deed,

And look no less, doth still create
About her, for her great thoughts breed
A calm that lifts us from our fallen state,
And makes us while with her both good and
  great—
Nor is their memory wanting in our need:
With stronger loving, every hour,
Turneth my heart to this frail flower,
Which, thoughtless of the world, hath
  grown
To beauty and meek gentleness,
Here in a fair world of its own—
By woman's instinct trained alone—
A lily fair which God did bless,
And which from Nature's heart did draw
Love, wisdom, peace, and Heaven's perfect law.

LOVE'S ALTAR.

I.

I BUILT an altar in my soul,
I builded it to one alone;
And ever silently I stole,
In happy days of long-agone,
To make rich offerings to that ONE.

II.

'Twas garlanded with purest thought,
And crowned with fancy's flowers bright,
With choicest gems 'twas all inwrought
Of truth and feeling; in my sight
It seemed a spot of cloudless light.

III.

Yet when I made my offering there,
Like Cain's, the incense would not rise;
Back on my heart down-sank the prayer,
And altar-stone and sacrifice
Grew hateful in my tear-dimmed eyes.

IV.

O'er-grown with age's mosses green,
The little altar firmly stands;
It is not, as it once hath been,
A selfish shrine;—these time-taught hands
Bring incense now from many lands.

V.

Knowledge doth only widen love;
The stream, that lone and narrow rose,
Doth, deepening ever, onward move,
And with an even current flows
Calmer and calmer to the close.

VI.

The love, that in those early days
Girt round my spirit like a wall,
Hath faded like a morning haze,
And flames, unpent by self's mean thrall,
Rise clearly to the perfect ALL.

MY LOVE.

I.

Not as all other women are
Is she that to my soul is dear;
Her glorious fancies come from **far**
Beneath the silver evening-star,
And yet her heart is ever near.

II.

Great feelings hath she of her own
Which lesser souls may never know;
God giveth them to her alone,
And sweet they are as any tone
Wherewith the wind may choose to **blow.**

III.

Yet in herself she dwelleth not,
Although no home were half so fair,
No simplest duty is forgot,
Life hath no dim and lowly spot
That doth not in her sunshine share.

IV.

She doeth little kindnesses,
Which most leave undone, or despise,
For naught that sets one heart at ease,
And giveth happiness or peace,
Is low-esteemèd in her eyes.

V.

She hath no scorn of common things,
And, though she seem of other birth,
Round us her heart entwines and clings,
And patiently she folds her wings
To tread the humble paths of earth.

VI.

Blessing she is : God made her so,
And deeds of week-day holiness
Fall from her noiseless as the snow,
Nor hath she ever chanced to know
That aught were easier than to bless.

VII.

She is most fair, and thereunto
Her life doth rightly harmonize ;
Feeling or thought that was not true
Ne'er made less beautiful the blue
Unclouded heaven of her eyes.

VIII.

On Nature she doth muse and brood
With such a still and love-clear eye—
She is so gentle and so good—
The very flowers in the wood
Do bless her with their sympathy.

IX.

She is a woman : one in whom
The spring-time of her childish years
Hath never lost its fresh perfume,

Though knowing well that life hath **room**
For many blights and many tears.

x.

And youth in her a home will **find,**
Where he may dwell eternally;
Her soul is not of that weak kind
Which better love the life behind
Than that which is, or is to be.

xi.

I love her with a love as still
As a broad river's peaceful might,
Which, by high tower and lowly **mill,**
Goes wandering at its own will,
And yet doth ever flow aright.

xii.

And, on its full, deep breast serene,
Like quiet isles my duties lie;
It flows around them and between,
And makes them fresh and fair and **green,**
Sweet homes wherein to live and die.

WITH A PRESSED FLOWER.

THIS little flower from afar
Hath come from other lands to thine;
For, once, its white and drooping **star**
Could see its shadow in the Rhine.

Perchance some fair-haired German maid
Hath plucked one from the self-same stalk,
And numbered over, half afraid,
Its petals in her evening walk.

"He loves me, loves me not," she cries;
" He loves me more than earth or Heaven,"
And then glad tears have filled her eyes
To find the number was uneven.

So, Love, my heart doth wander forth
To farthest lands beyond the sea,
And search the fairest spots of earth
To find sweet flowers of thought for thee

A type this tiny blossom is
Of what my heart doth every day,
Seeking for pleasant fantasies
To brood upon when thou 'rt away.

And thou must count its petals well,
Because it is a gift from me;
And the last one of all shall tell
Something I 've often told to thee.

But here at home, where we were born,
Thou wilt find flowers just as true,
Down bending every summer morn
With freshness of New England dew.

For Nature, ever right in love,
Hath given them the same sweet tongue,
Whether with German skies above,
Or here our granite rocks among.

IMPARTIALITY.

I.

I CANNOT say a scene is fair
Because it is beloved of thee,
But I shall love to linger there,
For sake of thy dear memory;
I would not be so coldly just
As to love only what I must.

II.

I cannot say a thought is good
Because thou foundest joy in it;
Each soul must choose its proper food
Which Nature hath decreed most fit;
But I shall ever deem it so
Because it made thy heart o'erflow.

III.

I love thee for that thou art fair;
And that thy spirit joys in aught
Createth a new beauty there,
With thine own dearest image fraught
And love, for others' sake that springs,
Gives half their charm to lovely things.

BELLEROPHON.

DEDICATED TO MY FRIEND, JOHN F. HEATH.

I.

I FEEL the bandages unroll
That bound my inward seeing;
Freed are the bright wings of my soul,
　Types of my godlike being:
High thoughts are swelling in my heart
　And rushing through my brain;
May I never more lose part
　In my soul's realm again!
All things fair, where'er they be,
In earth or air, in sky or sea,
I have loved them all, and taken
All within my throbbing breast;
No more my spirit can be shaken
From its calm and kingly rest!
Love hath shed its light around me,
Love hath pierced the shades that bound
　　me;
Mine eyes are opened, I can see
The universe's mystery,
　The mighty heart and core
　Of After and Before
I see, and I am weak no more!
　12

II.

Upward! upward evermore,
To Heaven's open gate I soar!
Little thoughts are far behind me,
Which, when custom weaves together,
All the nobler man can tether—
Cobwebs now no more can bind me!
Now fold thy wings a little while,
  My trancèd soul, and lie
At rest on this Calypso-isle
  That floats in mellow sky,
A thousand isles with gentle motion
Rock upon the sunset ocean;
A thousand isles of thousand hues,
How bright! how beautiful! how rare!
Into my spirit they infuse
A purer, a diviner air;
The earth is growing dimmer,
And now the last faint glimmer
  Hath faded from the hill;
But in my higher atmosphere
The sunlight streameth red and clear,
  Fringing the islets still;—
Love lifts us to the sunlight,
Though the whole world be dark;
Love, wide Love, is the *one* light,
All else is but a fading spark;
Love is the nectar which doth fill
Our soul's cup even to overflowing,
And, warming heart, and thought, and will,
Doth lie within us mildly glowing,
From its own centre raying out
Beauty and Truth on all without.

III.

Each on his golden throne,
Full royally, alone,
I see the stars above me,
With sceptre and with diadem;
Mildly they look down and love me,
For I have ever yet loved them,
I see their ever-sleepless eyes
Watching the growth of destinies;
Calm, sedate,
The eyes of Fate,
They wink not, nor do roll,
But search the depths of soul—
And in those mighty depths they see
The germs of all Futurity,
Waiting but the fitting time
To burst and ripen into prime,
As in the womb of mother Earth
The seeds of plants and forests lie
Age upon age and never die—
So in the souls of all men wait,
Undyingly the seeds of Fate;
Chance breaks the clod and forth they spring,
Filling blind men with wondering.
Eternal stars! with holy awe,
As if a present God I saw,
I look into those mighty eyes
And see great destinies arise,
As in those of mortal men
Feelings glow and fade again!
All things below, all things above,
Are open to the eyes of Love.

IV.

Of Knowledge Love is master-key,
Knowledge of Beauty ; passing dear
Is each to each, and mutually
Each one doth make the other clear;
Beauty is Love, and what we love
Straightway is beautiful,
So is the circle round and full,.
And so dear Love doth live and move
    And have his being,
Finding his proper food
    By sure inseeing,
In all things pure and good,
Which he at will doth cull,
Like a joyous butterfly
Hiving in the sunny bowers
Of the soul's fairest flowers,
Or, between the earth and sky,
Wandering at liberty
For happy, happy hours!

V.

The thoughts of Love are Poesy,
As this fair earth and all we see
Are the thoughts of Deity—
And Love is ours by our birthright!
He hath cleared mine inward sight;
Glorious shapes with glorious eyes
Round about my spirit glance,
Shedding a mild and golden light
On the shadowy face of Night;
To unearthly melodies,

Hand in hand, they weave their dance,
While a deep, ambrosial lustre
    From their rounded limbs doth shine,
Through many a rich and golden cluster
    Of streaming hair divine.
In our gross and earthly hours
We cannot see the Love-given powers
Which ever round the soul await
    To do its sovereign will,
When, in its moments calm and still,
It re-assumes its royal state,
Nor longer sits with eyes downcast,
A beggar, dreaming of the past,
At its own palace-gate.

VI.

    I too am a Maker and a Poet;
Through my whole soul I feel it and know it;
My veins are fired with ecstasy!
        All-mother Earth
        Did ne'er give birth
To one who shall be matched with me;
The lustre of my coronal
Shall cast a dimness over all.—
Alas! alas! what have I spoken?
My strong, my eagle wings are broken,
And back again to earth I fall!

SOMETHING NATURAL.

I.

WHEN first I saw thy soul-deep eyes,
My heart yearned to thee instantly,
Strange longing in my soul did rise;
I cannot tell the reason why,
But I must love thee till I die.

II.

The sight of thee hath well-nigh grown
As needful to me as the light;
I am unrestful when alone,
And my heart doth not beat aright
Except it dwell within thy sight.

III.

And yet—and yet—O selfish love!
I am not happy even with thee;
I see thee in thy brightness move,
And cannot well contented be,
Save thou should'st shine alone for me.

IV.

We should love beauty even as flowers—
For all, 'tis said, they bud and blow,
They are the world's as well as ours—
But thou—alas! God made thee grow
So fair, I cannot love thee so!

THE SYRENS.

The sea is lonely, the sea is dreary,
The sea is restless and uneasy;
Thou seekest quiet, thou art weary,
Wandering thou knowest not whither;—
Our little isle is green and breezy,
Come and rest thee! O come hither,
Come to this peaceful home of ours,
        Where evermore
The low west-wind creeps panting up the shore
To be at rest among the flowers;
Full of rest, the green moss lifts,
    As the dark waves of the sea
Draw in and out of rocky rifts
    Calling solemnly to thee,
With voices deep and hollow—
        To the shore
    Follow! O follow!
To be at rest for evermore!
        For evermore!

    Look how the gray old Ocean
From the depths of his heart rejoices,
Heaving with a gentle motion,
When he hears our restful voices:
List how he sings in an undertone,
Chiming with our melody;
And all sweet sounds of earth and air

Melt into one low voice alone,
That murmurs over the weary sea—
And seems to sing from everywhere—
" Here mayest thou harbour peacefully,
Here mayest thou rest from the aching oar
  Turn thy curvèd prow ashore,
And in our green isle rest for evermore!
    For evermore !
And Echo half wakes in the wooded hill,
  And, to her heart so calm and deep,
  Murmurs over in her sleep,
Doubtfully pausing and murmuring still,
    " Evermore ! "
          Thus, on Life's weary sea ;
          Heareth the marinere
          Voices sweet, from far and near,
          Ever singing low and clear,
          Ever singing longingly.

  Is it not better here to be,
Than to be toiling late and soon?
In the dreary night to see
Nothing but the blood-red moon
Go up and down into the sea;
Or, in the loneliness of day,
  To see the still seas only,
Solemnly lift their faces gray,
  Making it yet more lonely ?
Is it not better, than to hear
Only the sliding of the wave
Beneath the plank, and feel so near
A cold and lonely grave,
A restless grave, where thou shalt lie

Even in death unquietly?
Look down beneath thy wave-worn bark,
  Lean over the side and see
The leaden eye of the side-long shark
     Upturnèd patiently,
  Ever waiting there for thee:
Look down and see those shapeless forms,
  Which ever keep their dreamless sleep
  Far down within the gloomy deep,
And only stir themselves in storms,
Rising like islands from beneath,
And snorting through the angry spray,
As the frail vessel perisheth
In the whirls of their unwieldy play;
    Look down! Look down!
Upon the seaweed, slimy and dark,
That waves its arms so lank and brown,
    Beckoning for thee!
Look down beneath thy wave-worn bark
  Into the cold depth of the sea!
    Look down! Look down!
      Thus, on Life's lonely sea,
      Heareth the marinere
      Voices sad, from far and near,
      Ever singing full of fear,
      Ever singing drearfully.

Here all is pleasant as a dream;
The mind scarce shaketh down the dew,
The green grass floweth like a stream
  Into the ocean's blue:
    Listen! O listen!
Here is a gush of many streams,

A song of many birds,
And every wish and longing seems
Lulled to a numbered flow of words—
        Listen ! O listen !
Here ever hum the golden bees
Underneath full-blossomed trees,
At once with glowing fruit and flower
        crowned ;—
The sand is so smooth, the yellow sand,
That thy keel will not grate, as it touches the
        land;
All around, with a slumberous sound,
The singing waves slide up the strand,
And there, where the smooth wet pebbles be,
The waters gurgle longingly,
As if they fain would seek the shore,
To be at rest from the ceaseless roar,
To be at rest for evermore—
        For evermore.
            Thus, on Life's gloomy sea,
            Heareth the marinere
            Voices sweet, far and near,
            Ever singing in his ear,
        "Here is rest and peace for thee!"

Nantasket, July, 1840.

A FEELING.

THE flowers and the grass to me
Are eloquent reproachfully ;
For would they wave so pleasantly
Or look so fresh and fair,
If a man, cunning, hollow, mean,
Or one in anywise unclean,
Were looking on them there ?

   No ; he hath grown so foolish-wise
He cannot see with childhood's eyes;
He hath forgot that purity
And lowliness which are the key
Of Nature's mysteries ;
No ; he hath wandered off so long
From his own place of birth,
That he hath lost his mother-tongue,
And, like one come from far-off lands,
Forgetting and forgot, he stands
Beside his mother's hearth.

THE BEGGAR.

A BEGGAR through the world am I,
From place to place I wander by ;—
Fill up my pilgrim's scrip for me,
For Christ's sweet sake and charity!

A little of thy steadfastness,
Rounded with leafy gracefulness,
Old oak, give me—
That the world's blasts may round me blow,
And I yield gently to and fro,
While my stout-hearted trunk below
And firm-set roots unmovèd be.

Some of thy stern, unyielding might,
Enduring still through day and night
Rude tempest-shock and withering blight—
That I may keep at bay
The changeful April sky of chance
And the strong tide of circumstance—
Give me, old granite gray.

Some of thy mournfulness serene,
Some of thy never-dying green,
Put in this scrip of mine—
That grief may fall like snowflakes light,
And deck me in a robe of white,
Ready to be an angel bright—
O sweetly-mournful pine.

A little of thy merriment,
Of thy sparkling, light content,
Give me my cheerful brook—
That I may still be full of glee
And gladsomeness, where'er I be,
Though fickle fate hath prisoned me
In some neglected nook.

Ye have been very kind and good
To me, since I 've been in the wood;
Ye have gone nigh to fill my heart;
But good-bye, kind friends, every one,
I 've far to go ere set of sun;
Of all good things I would have part,
The day was high ere I could start,
And so my journey's scarce begun.

Heaven help me! how could I forget
To beg of thee, dear violet!
Some of thy modesty,
That flowers here as well, unseen,
As if before the world thou 'dst been,
O give, to strengthen me.

SERENADE.

From the close-shut windows gleams no spark,
The night is chilly, the night is dark,
The poplars shiver, the pine-trees moan,
My hair by the autumn breeze is blown,
Under thy window I sing alone,
Alone, alone, ah woe! alone!

The darkness is pressing coldly around,
The windows shake with a lonely sound,
The stars are hid and the night is drear,
The heart of silence throbs in thine ear,
In thy chamber thou sittest alone,
Alone, alone, ah woe! alone!

The world is happy, the world is wide,
Kind hearts are beating on every side;
Ah, why should we lie so curled
Alone in the shell of this great world?
Why should we any more be alone?
Alone, alone, ah woe! alone!

O! 'tis a bitter and dreary word,
The saddest by man's ear ever heard;
We each are young, we each have a heart,
Why stand we ever coldly apart?
Must we forever, then, be alone?
Alone, alone, ah woe! alone!

IRENE.

Hers is a spirit deep and crystal-clear;
Calmly beneath her earnest face it lies,
Free without boldness, meek without a fear,
Quicker to look than speak its sympathies;
Far down into her large and patient eyes
I gaze, deep-drinking of the infinite,
As, in the mid-watch of a clear, still night,
I look into the fathomless blue skies.

So circled lives she with Love's holy light,
That from the shade of self she walketh free;
The garden of her soul still keepeth she
An Eden where the snake did never enter;
She hath a natural, wise sincerity,
A simple truthfulness, and these have lent her
A dignity as moveless as the centre;
So that no influence of earth can stir
Her steadfast courage, or can take away
The holy peacefulness, which, night and day,
Unto her queenly soul doth minister.

Most gentle is she; her large charity
(An all unwitting, childlike gift in her)
Not freer is to give than meek to bear;
And, though herself not unacquaint with care,
Hath in her heart wide room for all that be—
Her heart that hath no secrets of its own,
But open is as eglantine full-blown,
Cloudless forever is her brow serene,
Speaking calm hope and trust within her,
    whence
Welleth a noiseless spring of patience
That keepeth all her life so fresh, so green
And full of holiness, that every look,
The greatness of her woman's soul revealing,
Unto me bringeth blessing, and a feeling
As when I read in God's own holy book.

A graciousness in giving that doth make
The small'st gift greatest, and a sense most
    meek
Of worthiness, that doth not fear to take

From others, but which always fears to speak
Its thanks in utterance, for the giver's sake;—
The deep religion of a thankful heart,
Which rests instinctively with Heaven's law
With a full peace, that never can depart
From its own steadfastness;—a holy awe
For holy things, not those which men call holy,
But such as are revealèd to the eyes
Of a true woman's soul bent down and lowly
Before the face of daily mysteries;—
A love that blossoms soon, but ripens slowly
To the full goldenness of fruitful prime,
Enduring with a firmness that defies
All shallow tricks of circumstance and time,
By a sure insight knowing where to cling,
And where it clingeth never withering—
These are Irene's dowry—which no fate
Can shake from their serene, deep-builded
    state.

In-seeing sympathy is hers, which chasteneth
No less loveth, scorning to be bound
With fear of blame, and yet which ever hast-
    eneth
To pour the balm of kind looks on the wound,
If they be wounds which such sweet teaching
    makes,
Giving itself a pang for others' sakes;
No want of faith, that chills with side-long eye,
Hath she; no jealousy, no Levite pride
That passeth by upon the other side;
For in her soul there never dwelt a lie,
Right from the hand of God her spirit came

Unstained, and she hath ne'er forgotten whence
It came, nor wandered far from thence,
But laboreth to keep her still the same,
Near to her place of birth, that she may not
Soil her white raiment with an earthly spot.

Yet sets she not her soul so steadily
Above, that she forgets her ties to earth,
But her whole thought would almost seem to be
How to make glad one lowly human hearth;
For with a gentle courage she doth strive
In thought and word and feeling so to live
As to make earth next Heaven; and her heart
Herein doth show its most exceeding worth,
That, bearing in our frailty her just part,
She hath not shrunk from evils of this life,
But hath gone calmly forth into the strife,
And all its sins and sorrows hath withstood
With lofty strength of patient womanhood:
For this I love her great soul more than all,
That, being bound, like us, with earthly thrall,
She walks so bright and Heaven-wise therein—
Too wise, too meek, too womanly to sin.

Exceeding pleasant to mine eyes is she;
Like a lone star through riven storm-clouds seen
By sailors, tempest-tost upon the sea,
Telling of rest and peaceful havens nigh,
Unto my soul her star-like soul hath been,
Her sight as full of hope and calm to me;—
For she unto herself hath builded high
A home serene, wherein to lay her head,
Earth's noblest thing—a Woman perfected.

13

THE LOST CHILD.

I.

I WANDERED down the sunny glade
  And ever mused, my love, of thee;
My thoughts, like little children, played,
  As gaily and as guilelessly.

II.

If any chanced to go astray,
  Moaning in fear of coming harms,
Hope brought the wanderer back alway,
  Safe nestled in her snowy arms.

III.

From that soft nest the happy one
  Looked up at me and calmly smiled;
Its hair shone golden in the sun,
  And made it seem a heavenly child.

IV.

Dear Hope's blue eyes smiled mildly down,
  And blest it with a love so deep,
That, like a nurseling of her own,
  It clasped her neck and fell asleep.

THE CHURCH.

I.

I LOVE the rites of England's church;
  I love to hear and see
The priest and people reading slow
  The solemn Litany;
I love to hear the glorious swell
  Of chanted psalm and prayer,
And the deep organ's bursting heart,
  Throb through the shivering air.

II.

Chants, that a thousand years have heard,
  I. love to hear again,
For visions of the olden time
  Are wakened by the strain;
With gorgeous hues the window-glass
  Seems suddenly to glow
And rich and red the streams of light
  Down through the chancel flow.

III.

And then I murmur, "Surely God
  Delighteth here to dwell;
This is the temple of his Son
  Whom he doth love so well;"
But, when I hear the creed which saith,
  This church alone is His,

I feel within my soul that He
　　Hath purer shrines than this.

IV.

For his is not the builded church,
　　Nor organ-shaken dome;
In every thing that lovely is
　　He loves and hath his home;
And most in soul that loveth well
　　All things which he hath made,
Knowing no creed but simple faith
　　That may not be gainsaid.

V.

His church is universal Love,
　　And whoso dwells therein
Shall need no customed sacrifice
　　To wash away his sin;
And music in its aisles shall swell,
　　Of lives upright and true,
Sweet as dreamed sounds of angel-harps
　　Down-quivering through the blue.

VI.

They shall not ask a litany,
　　The souls that worship there,
But every look shall be a hymn,
　　And every word a prayer;
Their service shall be written bright
　　In calm and holy eyes,
And every day from fragrant hearts
　　Fit incense shall arise.

THE UNLOVELY.

THE pretty things that others wear
Look strange and out of place on me,
I never seem dressed tastefully,
   Because I am not fair;
And, when I would most pleasing seem,
And deck myself with joyful care,
I find it is an idle dream,
   Because I am not fair.

If I put roses in my hair,
They bloom as if in mockery;
Nature denies her sympathy,
   Because I am not fair;
Alas! I have a warm, true heart,
But when I show it people stare;
I must forever dwell apart,
   Because I am not fair.

I am least happy being where
The hearts of others are most light,
And strive to keep me out of sight,
   Because I am not fair;
The glad ones often give a glance,
As I am sitting lonely there,
That asks me why I do not dance—
   Because I am not fair.

And if to smile on them I dare,
For that my heart with love runs o'er,
They say: " What *is* she laughing for?"—
   Because I am not fair;
Love scorned or misinterpreted—
It is the hardest thing to bear;
I often wish that I were dead,
   Because I am not fair.

In joy or grief I must not share,
For neither smiles nor tears on me
Will ever look becomingly,
   Because I am not fair;
Whole days I sit alone and cry,
And in my grave I wish I were—
Yet none will weep me if I die,
   Because I am not fair.

My grave will be so lone and bare,
I fear to think of those dark hours,
For none will plant it o'er with flowers,
   Because I am not fair;
They will not in the summer come
And speak kind words above me there;
To me the grave will be no home,
   Because I am not fair.

LOVE-SONG.

NEARER to thy mother-heart,
Simple Nature, press me,
Let me know thee as thou art,
Fill my soul and bless me!
I have loved thee long and well,
I have loved thee heartily;
Shall I never with thee dwell,
Never be at one with thee?

Inward, inward to thy heart,
Kindly Nature, take me,
Lovely even as thou art,
Full of loving make me!
Thou knowest naught of dead-cold forms,
Knowest naught of littleness,
Lifeful Truth thy being warms,
Majesty and earnestness.

Homeward, homeward to thy heart,
Dearest Nature, call me;
Let no halfness, no mean part,
Any longer thrall me!
I will be thy lover true,
Will be a faithful soul,
Then circle me, then look me through,
Fill me with the mighty Whole.

SONG.

ALL things are sad :—
I go and ask of Memory,
That she tells sweet tales to me
  To make me glad ;
And she takes me by the hand,
  Leadeth to old places,
  Showeth the old faces
In her hazy mirage-land ;
O, her voice is sweet and low,
And her eyes are fresh to mine
      As the dew
      Gleaming through
The half-unfolded Eglantine,
Long ago, long ago !
But I feel that I am only
Yet more sad, and yet more lonely!

Then I turn to blue-eyed Hope,
And beg of her that she will ope
Her golden gates for me ;
She is fair and full of grace,
But she hath the form and face
Of her mother Memory ;
Clear as air her glad voice ringeth,
Joyous are the songs she singeth,
Yet I hear them mournfully ;—
They are songs her mother taught her,
Crooning to her infant daughter,

As she lay upon her knee.
Many little ones she bore me,
Woe is me! in by-gone hours,
Who danced along and sang before me,
Scattering my way with flowers;
       One by one
      They are gone,
And their silent graves are seen,
Shining fresh with mosses green,
Where the rising sunbeams slope
O'er the dewy land of Hope.
  But, when sweet Memory faileth,
And Hope looks strange and cold;
When youth no more availeth,
And Grief grows over bold; —
When softest winds are dreary,
And summer sunlight weary,
And sweetest things uncheery
      We know not why:—
When the crown of our desires
Weighs upon the brow and tires,
     And we would die,
Die for, ah! we know not what,
Something we seem to have forgot,
Something we had, and now have not;—
When the present is a weight
And the future seems our foe,
And with shrinking eyes we wait,
As one who dreads a sudden blow
In the dark, he knows not whence;—
When Love at last his bright eye closes,
And the bloom upon his face,
That lends him such a living grace,

Is a shadow from the roses
Wherewith we have decked his bier,
Because he once was passing dear ;—
When we feel a leaden sense
Of nothingness and impotence,
    Till we grow mad—
    Then the body saith,
      "There's but one true faith
      All things are sad!"

A LOVE-DREAM.

PLEASANT thoughts come wandering,
When thou art far, from thee to me;
On their silver wings they bring
A very peaceful ecstasy,
A feeling of eternal spring;
So that Winter half forgets
Everything but that thou art,
And, in his bewildered heart,
Dreameth of the violets,
Or those bluer flowers that ope,
Flowers of steadfast love and hope,
Watered by the living wells,
Of memories dear, and dearer prophecies
When young spring forever dwells
In the sunshine of thine eyes.

I have most holy dreams of thee,
  All night I have such dreams;

And, when I awake, reality
  No whit the darker seems;
Through the twin gates of Hope and Memory
  They pour in crystal streams
  From out an angel's calmèd eyes,
  Who, from twilight till sunrise,
  Far away in the upper deep,
  Poised upon his shining wings,
  Over us his watch doth keep,
  And, as he watcheth, ever sings.

  Through the still night I hear him sing,
    Down-looking on our sleep;
  I hear his clear, clear harp-strings ring,
  And, as the golden notes take wing,
  Gently downward hovering,
    For very joy I weep;
  He singeth songs of holy Love,
  That quiver through the depths afar,
  Where the blessèd spirits are,
  And lingeringly from above
  Shower till the morning star
  His silver shield hath buckled on
  And sentinels the dawn alone,
  Quivering his gleamy spear
  Through the dusky atmosphere.

  Almost, my love, I fear the morn,
  When that blessèd voice shall cease,
  Lest it should leave me quite forlorn,
  Stript of my snowy robe of peace;
  And yet the bright reality

Is fairer than all dreams can be,
For, through my spirit, all day long,
Ring echoes of that angel-song
In melodious thoughts of thee ;
And well I know it cannot die
Till eternal morn shall break,
For, through life's slumber, thou and l
Will keep it for each other's sake,
And it shall not be silent when we wake.

FOURTH OF JULY ODE.

I.

OUR fathers fought for Liberty,
They struggled long and well,
History of their deeds can tell—
But did they leave us free ?

II.

Are we free from vanity,
Free from pride, and free from self,
Free from love of power and self,
From everything that 's beggarly ?

III.

Are we free from stubborn will,
From low hate and malice small,
From opinion's tyrant thrall ?
Are none of us our own slaves still ?

IV.

Are we free to speak our thought,
To be happy, and be poor,
Free to enter Heaven's door,
To live and labor as we ought?

V.

Are we then made free at last
From the fear of what men say,
Free to reverence To-day,
Free from the slavery of the Past?

VI.

Our fathers fought for liberty,
They struggled long and well,
History of their deeds can tell—
But *ourselves* must set us free.

SPHINX.

I.

WHY mourn we for the golden prime
When our young souls *were* kingly, strong, and
true?
The soul is greater than all time,
It changes not, but yet is ever new.

II.

But that the soul *is* noble, we
Could never know what nobleness had been;
Be what ye dream! and earth shall see
A greater greatness than she e'er hath seen.

III.

The flower pines not to be fair,
It never asketh to be sweet and dear,
But gives itself to sun and air,
And so is fresh and full from year to year.

IV.

Nothing in Nature weeps its lot,
Nothing, save man, abides in memory,
Forgetful that the Past is what
Ourselves may choose the coming time to be.

V.

All things are circular; the Past
Was given us to make the Future great;
And the void Future shall at last
Be the strong rudder of an after fate.

VI.

We sit beside the Sphinx of Life,
We gaze into its void, unanswering eyes,
And spend ourselves in idle strife
To read the riddle of their mysteries.

VII.

Arise! be earnest and be strong!
The Sphinx's eyes shall suddenly grow clear,
And speak as plain to thee ere long,
As the dear maiden's who holds thee most dear.

VIII.

The meaning of all things in *us*—
Yea, in the lives we give our souls—doth lie;

Make, then, their meaning glorious
By such a life as need not fear to die!

IX.

There is no heart-beat in the day,
Which bears a record of the smallest deed,
But holds within its faith alway
That which in doubt we vainly strive to read.

X.

One seed contains another seed,
And that a third, and so for evermore;
And promise of as great a deed
Lies folded in the deed that went before.

XI.

So ask not fitting space or time,
Yet could not dream of things which could not
be ;
Each day shall make the next sublime,
And Time be swallowed in Eternity.

XII.

God bless the Present! it is ALL;
It has been Future, and it shall be Past;
Awake and live! thy strength recall,
And in one trinity unite them fast.

XIII.

Action and Life—lo! here the key
Of all on earth that seemeth dark and wrong;
Win this—and, with it, freely ye
May enter that bright realm for which ye long.

XIV.

Then all these bitter questionings
Shall with a full and blessèd answer meet;
Past worlds, whereof the Poet sings,
Shall be the earth beneath his snow-white fleet.

"GOE, LITTLE BOOKE!"

Go LITTLE book! the world is wide,
There's room and verge enough for thee;
For thou hast learned that only pride
Lacketh fit opportunity,
Which comes unbid to modesty.
   Go! win thy way with gentleness:
I send thee forth, my first-born child,
Quite, quite alone, to face the stress
Of fickle skies and pathways wild,
Where few can keep them undefiled.
   Thou camest from a poet's heart,
A warm, still home, and full of rest;
Far from the pleasant eyes thou art
Of those who know and love thee best,
And by whose hearthstones thou wert blest.
   Go! knock thou softly at the door
Where any gentle spirits bin,
Tell them thy tender feet are sore,
Wandering so far from all thy kin,
And ask if thou may enter in.
   Beg thou a cup-full from the spring
Of Charity, in Christ's dear name;

Few will deny so small a thing,
Nor ask unkindly if thou came
Of one whose life might do thee shame.
  We all are prone to go astray,
Our hopes are bright, our lives are dim;
But thou art pure, and if they say,
"We know thy father, and our whim
He pleases not,"—plead thou for him.
  For many are by whom all truth,
That speaks not in their mother-tongue,
Is stoned to death with hands unruth,
Or hath its patient spirit wrung
Cold words and colder looks among.
  Yet fear not! for skies are fair
To all whose souls are fair within;
Thou wilt find shelter everywhere
With those to whom a different skin
Is not a damning proof of sin.
  But, if all others are unkind,
There 's *one* heart whither thou canst fly
For shelter from the biting wind;
And, in that home of purity,
It were no bitter thing to die.
  14

SONNETS.

I.

DISAPPOINTMENT.

I PRAY thee call not this society;
I asked for bread; thou givest me a stone;
I am an hungered, and I find not one
To give me meat, to joy or grieve with me;
I find not here what I went out to see—
Souls of true men, of women who can move
The deeper, better part of us to love,
Souls that can hold with mine communion
  free.
Alas! must then these hopes, these longings
  high,
This yearning of the soul for brotherhood,
And all that makes us pure, and wise, and
  good,
Come broken-hearted, home again to die?
No, Hope is left, and prays with bended head,
"Give us this day, O God, our daily bread!"

II.

GREAT human nature, whither art thou fled?
Are these things creeping forth and back
  agen,
These hollow formalists and echoes, men?

Art thou entombed with the mighty dead?
In God's name, no! not yet hath all been said,
Or done, or longed for, that is truly great;
These pitiful dried crusts will never sate
Natures for which pure Truth is daily bread;
We were not meant to plod along the earth,
Strange to ourselves and to our fellows
    strange;
We were not meant to struggle from our birth,
To skulk and creep, and in mean pathways
    range;
Act! with stern truth, large faith, and loving
    will!
Up and be doing! God is with us still.

III.

TO A FRIEND.

ONE strip of bark may feed the broken tree,
Giving to some few limbs a sickly green;
And one light shower on the hills, I ween,
May keep the spring from drying utterly.
Thus seemeth it with these our hearts to be;
Hope is the strip of bark, the shower of rain,
And so they are not wholly crushed with pain.
But live and linger on, for sadder sight to see,
Much do they err, who tell us that the heart
May not be broken; what, then, can we call
A broken heart, if this may not be so,
This death in life when, shrouded in its pall,
Shunning and shunned, it dwelleth all apart,
Its power, its love, its sympathy laid low?

IV.

So MAY it be, but let it not be so,
O, let it not be so with thee, my friend;
Be of good courage, bear up to the end,
And on thine after way rejoicing go!
We all must suffer, if we aught would know;
Life is a teacher stern, and wisdom's crown
Is oft a crown of thorns, whence, trickling down,
Blood, mixed with tears, blinding her eyes doth
    flow;
But Time, a gentle nurse, shall wipe away
This bloody sweat, and thou shalt find on earth,
That woman is not all in all to Love,
But, living by a new and second birth,
Thy soul shall see all things below, above,
Grow bright and brighter to the perfect day.

V.

O CHILD of Nature! O most meek and free,
Most gentle spirit of true nobleness!
Thou doest not a worthy deed the less
Because the world may not its greatness see;
What were a thousand triumphings to thee,
Who, in thyself, art as a perfect sphere
Wrapt in a bright and natural atmosphere
Of mighty-souledness and majesty?
Thy soul is not too high for lowly things,
Feels not its strength seeing its brother weak,
Not for itself unto itself is dear,
But for that it may guide the wanderings
Of fellow-men, and to their spirits speak
The lofty faith of heart that knows no fear.

VI.

" For this true nobleness I seek in vain,
In woman and in man I find it not,
I almost weary of my earthly lot,
My life-springs are dried up with burning
 pain."—
Thou find'st it not? I pray thee look again,
Look *inward* through the depths of thine own
 soul;
How is it with thee? Art thou sound and
 whole?
Doth narrow search show thee no earthly stain?
BE NOBLE ! and the nobleness that lies
In other men, sleeping but never dead,
Will rise in majesty to meet thine own;
Then wilt thou see it gleam in many eyes,
Then will pure light around thy path be shed,
And thou wilt nevermore be sad and lone.

VII.

TO ———

DEEM it no Sodom-fruit of vanity,
Or fickle fantasy of unripe youth
Which ever takes the fairest shows for truth,
That I should wish my verse beloved of thee;
'Tis love's deep thirst which may not quenchèd
 be.
There is a gulf of longing and unrest,
A wild love-craving not to be represt,
Whereto, in all our hearts, as to the sea,
The streams of feeling do forever flow.
Therefore it is that thy well-meted praise

Falleth so shower-like and fresh on me,
Filling those springs which else had sunk full
    low,
Lost in the dreary desert-sands of woe,
Or parched by passion's fierce and withering
    blaze.

VIII.

MIGHT I but be beloved, and, O most fair
And perfect-ordered soul, beloved of thee,
How should I feel a cloud of earthly care,
If thy blue eyes were ever clear to me?
O woman's love! O flower most bright and
    rare!
That blossom'st brightest in extremest need,
Woe, woe is me! that thy so precious seed
Is ever sown by Fancy's changeful air,
And grows sometimes in poor and barren hearts,
Who can be little even in the light
Of thy meek holiness—while souls more great
Are left to wander in a starless night,
Praying unheard—and yet the hardest parts
Befit those best who best can cope with fate.

IX.

WHY should we ever weary of this life?
Our souls should widen ever, not contract,
Grow stronger, and not harder, in the strife,
Filling each moment with a noble act;
If we live thus, of vigor all compact,
Doing our duty to our fellow-men,
And striving rather to exalt our race
Than our poor selves, with earnest hand or pen

We shall erect our names a dwelling-place
Which not all ages shall cast down agen;
Offspring of Time shall then be born each hour,
Which, as of old, earth lovingly shall guard,
To live forever in youth's perfect flower,
And guide her future children Heavenward.

X.

GREEN MOUNTAINS.

YE mountains, that far off lift up your heads,
Seen dimly through their canopies of blue,
The shade of my unrestful spirit sheds
Distance-created beauty over you;
I am not well content with this far view;
How may I know what foot of loved-one treads
Your rocks moss-grown and sun-dried torrent
    beds ?
We should love all things better, if we knew
What claims the meanest have upon our hearts:
Perchance even now some eye, that would be
    bright
To meet my own, looks on your mist-robed
    forms;
Perchance your grandeur a deep joy imparts
To souls that have encircled mine with light—
O brother-heart, with thee my spirit warms!

XI.

My friend, adown Life's valley, hand in hand,
With grateful change of grave and merry
    speech
Or song, our hearts unlocking each to each,

We 'll journey onward to the silent land;
And when stern Death shall loose that loving
     band,
Taking in his cold hand a hand of ours,
The one shall strew the other's grave with
     flowers,
Nor shall his heart a moment be unmanned.
My friend and brother! if thou goest first,
Wilt thou no more re-visit me below ?
Yea, when my heart seems happy causelessly
And swells, not dreaming why, as it would
     burst
With joy unspeakable—my soul shall know
That thou, unseen, art bending over me.

XII.

Verse cannot say how beautiful thou art,
How glorious the calmness of thine eyes,
Full of unconquerable energies,
Telling that thou hast acted well thy part.
No doubt or fear thy steady faith can start,
No thought of evil dare come nigh to thee,
Who hast the courage meek of purity,
The self-stayed greatness of a loving heart,
Strong with serene, enduring fortitude ;
Where'er thou art, that seems thy fitting place,
For not of forms, but Nature, art thou child;
And lowest things put on a noble grace
When touched by ye, O patient, Ruth-like,
     mild
And spotless hands of earnest womanhood.

XIII.

THE soul would fain its loving kindness tell,
But custom hangs like lead upon the tongue;
The heart is brimful, hollow crowds among,
When it finds one whose life and thought are
    well;
Up to the eyes its gushing love doth swell,
The angel cometh and the waters move,
Yet is it fearful still to say " I love,"
And words come grating as a jangled bell.
O might we only speak but what we feel,
Might the tongue pay but what the heart doth
    owe,
Not Heaven's great thunder, when, deep peal
    on peal,
It shakes the earth, could rouse our spirits so,
Or to the soul such majesty reveal,
As two short words half-spoken faint and low!

XIV.

I SAW a gate : a harsh voice spake and said,
" This is the gate of Life ; " above was writ,
" Leave hope behind, all ye who enter it ; "
Then shrank my heart within itself for dread;
But, softer than the summer rain is shed,
Words dropt upon my soul, and they did say,
" Fear nothing, Faith shall save thee, watch
    and pray ! "
So, without fear I lifted up my head,
And lo! that writing was not, one fair word
Was carven in its stead, and it was " Love."

Then rained once more those sweet tones from
    above
With healing on their wings: I humbly heard,
"I am the Life, ask and it shall be given!
I am the way, by me ye enter Heaven!"

XV.

I WOULD not have this perfect love of ours
Grow from a single root, a single stem,
Bearing no goodly fruit, but only flowers
That idly hide Life's iron diadem:
It should grow alway like that Eastern tree
Whose limbs take root and spread forth con-
    stantly;
That love for one, from which there doth not
    spring
Wide love for all, is but a worthless thing.
Not in another world, as poets prate,
Dwell we apart, above the tide of things,
High floating o'er earth's clouds on faery wings;
But our pure love doth ever elevate
Into a holy bond of brotherhood
All earthly things, making them pure and good.

XVI.

To THE dark, narrow house where loved ones
    go,
Whence no steps outward turn, whose silent
    door
None but the sexton knocks at any more,
Are they not sometimes with us yet below?
The longings of the soul would tell us so;

Although, so pure and fine their being's essence,
Our bodily eyes are witless of their presence,
Yet not within the tomb their spirits glow,
Like wizard lamps pent up, but whensoever
With great thoughts worthy of their high be-
      hests
Our souls are filled, those bright ones with us
      be,
As, in the patriarch's tent, his angel guests;—
O let us live so worthily, that never
We may be far from that blest company.

XVII.

I FAIN would give to thee the loveliest things,
For lovely things belong to thee of right,
And thou hast been as peaceful to my sight,
As the still thoughts that summer twilight
      brings ;
Beneath the shadow of thine angel wings
O let me live!   O let me rest in thee,
Growing to thee more and more utterly,
Upbearing and upborn, till outward things
Are only as they share in thee a part!
Look kindly on me, let thy holy eyes
Bless me from the deep fulness of thy heart;
So shall my soul in its right strength arise,
And nevermore shall pine and shrink and start,
Safe-sheltered in thy full souled sympathies.

XVIII.

MUCH I had mused of Love, and in my soul
There was one chamber where I dared not look,
So much its dark and dreary voidness shook

My spirit, feeling that I was not whole:
All my deep longings flowed toward one goal
For long, long years, but were not answerèd,
Till Hope was drooping, Faith well-nigh stone·
    dead,
And I was still a blind, earth-delving mole;
Yet did I know that God was wise and good,
And would fulfill my being,late or soon;
Nor was such thought in vain, for, seeing thee,
Great Love rose up, as, o'er a black pine wood,
Round, bright, and clear, upstarteth the full
    moon,
Filling my soul with glory utterly.

XIX.

SAYEST thou, most beautiful, that thou wilt
    wear
Flowers and leafy crowns when thou art old,
And that thy heart shall never grow so cold
But they shall love to wreath thy silvered hair
And into age's snows the hope of spring-tide
    bear?
O, in thy childlike wisdom's moveless hold
Dwell ever! still the blessings manifold
Of purity, of peace, and untaught care
For other's hearts, around thy pathway shed,
And thou shalt have a crown of deathless
    flowers
To glorify and guard thy blessed head
And give their freshness to thy life's last hours;
And, when the Bridegroom calleth, they shall be
A wedding-garment white as snow for thee.

XX.

Poet! who sittest in thy pleasant room,
Warming thy heart with idle thoughts of love,
And of a holy life that leads above,
Striving to keep life's spring-flower still in
    bloom,
And lingering to snuff their fresh perfume—
O, there were other duties meant for thee,
Than to sit down in peacefulness and Be!
O, there are brother-hearts that dwell in gloom,
Souls loathsome, foul, and black with daily sin,
So crusted o'er with baseness, that no ray
Of heaven's blessed light may enter in!
Come down, then, to the hot and dusty way,
And lead them back to hope and peace again—
For, save in Act, thy Love is all in vain.

XXI.

" NO MORE BUT SO ? "

No more but so? Only with uncold looks,
And with a hand not laggard to clasp mine,
Think'st thou to pay what debt of love is thine?
No more but so? Like gushing water-brooks,
Freshening and making green the dimmest
    nooks
Of thy friend's soul thy kindliness should flow;
But, if 't is bounded by not saying " no,"
I can find more of friendship in my books,
All lifeless though they be, and more, far more
In every simplest moss, or flower, or tree;
Open to me thy heart of hearts' deep core,
Or never say that I am dear to thee;

Call me not Friend, if thou keep close the door
That leads into thine inmost sympathy.

XXII.

TO A VOICE HEARD IN MOUNT AUBURN.

LIKE the low warblings of a leaf-hid bird,
Thy voice came to me through the screening
      trees,
Singing the simplest, long-known melodies ;
I had no glimpse of thee, and yet I heard
And blest thee for each clearly-carolled word ;
I longed to thank thee, and my heart would
      frame
Mary or Ruth, some sisterly, sweet name
For thee, yet could I not my lips have stirred;
I knew that thou wert lovely, that thine eyes
Were blue and downcast, and methought large
      tears,
Unknown to thee, up to their lids must rise
With half-sad memories of other years,
As to thyself alone thou sangest o'er
Words that to childhood seemed to say " No
      More ! "

XXIII.

ON READING SPENSER AGAIN.

DEAR, gentle Spenser ! thou my soul dost lead,
A little child again, through Fairy land,
By many a bower and stream of golden sand,
And many a sunny plain whose light doth breed
A sunshine in my happy heart, and feed
My fancy with sweet visions ; I become

A knight, and with my charmèd arms would
    roam
To seek for fame in many a wondrous deed
Of high emprize—for I have seen the light
Of Una's angel's face, the golden hair
And backward eyes of startled Florimel;
And, for their holy sake, I would outdare
A host of cruel Paynims in the fight,
Or Archimage and all the powers of Hell.

XXIV.

LIGHT of mine eyes! with thy so trusting look,
And thy sweet smile of charity and love,
That from a treasure well uplaid above,
And from a hope in Christ its blessing took;
Light of my heart! which, when it could not
    brook
The coldness of another's sympathy,
Finds ever a deep peace and stay in thee,
Warm as the sunshine of a mossy nook;
Light of my soul! who, by thy saintliness
And faith that acts itself in daily life,
Canst raise me above weakness, and canst
    bless
The hardest thraldom of my earthly strife—
I dare not say how much thou art to me
'Even to myself—and O, far less to thee!

XXV.

SILENT as one who treads on new-fallen snow,
Love came upon me ere I was aware;
Not light of heart, for there was troublous
    care

Upon his eyelids, drooping them full low,
As with sad memory of a healèd woe;
The cold rain shivered in his golden hair,
As if an outcast lot had been his share,
And he seemed doubtful whither he should go:
Then he fell on my neck, and, in my breast
Hiding his face, awhile sobbed bitterly,
As half in grief to be so long distrest,
And half in joy at his security—
At last, uplooking from his place of rest,
His eyes shone blessedness and hope on me.

XXVI.

A GENTLENESS that grows of steady faith;
A joy that sheds its sunshine everywhere;
A humble strength and readiness to bear
Those burthens which strict duty ever lay'th
Upon our souls;—which unto sorrow saith,
" Here is no soil for thee to strike thy roots,
Here only grow those sweet and precious
    fruits;
Which ripen for the soul that well obey'th
A patience which the world can neither give
Nor take away ; a courage strong and high,
That dares in simple usefulness to live,
And without one sad look behind to die
When that day comes;—these tell me that our
    love
Is building for itself a home above.

XXVII.

WHEN the glad soul is full to overflow,
Unto the tongue all power it denies,

And only trusts its secret to the eyes;
For, by an inborn wisdom it doth know
There is no other eloquence but so;
And, when the tongue's weak utterance doth
    suffice,
Prisoned within the body's cell it lies,
Remembering in tears its exiled woe:
That word which all mankind so long to hear,
Which bears the spirit back to whence it came,
Maketh this sullen clay as crystal clear,
And will not be enclouded in a name;
It is a truth which we can feel and see,
But is as boundless as Eternity.

XXVIII.

TO THE EVENING-STAR.

When we have once said lowly " Evening-
    Star ! "
Words give no more—for, in thy silver pride,
Thou shinest as nought else can shine beside:
The thick smoke, coiling round the sooty bar
Forever, and the customed lamp-light mar
The stillness of my thought—seeing things
    glide
So samely :—then I ope my windows wide,
And gaze in peace to where thou shin'st afar,
The wind that comes across the faint-white
    snow
So freshly, and the river dimly seen,
Seem like new things that never had been so.
Before ; and thou art bright as thou hast been
Since thy white rays put sweetness in the eyes
Of the first souls that loved in Paradise

15

XXIX.

READING.

As one who on some well-known landscape
    looks,
Be it alone, or with some dear friend nigh,
Each day beholdeth fresh variety,
New harmonies of hills, and trees, and brooks—
So is it with the worthiest choice of books,
And oftenest read : if thou no meaning spy,
Deem there is meaning wanting in thine eyes;
We are so lured from judgment by the crooks
And winding ways of covert fantasy,
Or turned unwittingly down beaten tracks
Of our foregone conclusions, that we see,
In our own want, the writer's misdeemed lacks:
It is with true books as with Nature, each
New day of living doth new insight teach.

XXX.

TO ——, AFTER A SNOW-STORM.

BLUE as thine eyes the river gently flows
Between his banks, which, far as eye can see,
Are whiter than aught else on earth may be,
Save inmost thoughts that in thy soul repose;
The trees, all crystalled by the melted snows,
Sparkle with gems and silver, such as we
In childhood saw 'mong groves of Faërie,
And the dear skies are sunny-blue as those ;
Still as thy heart, when next mine own it lies
In love's full safety, is the bracing air ;
The earth is all enwrapt with draperies

Snow-white as that pure love might choose to
  wear—
O for one moment's look into thine eyes,
To share the joy such scene would kindle there!

SONNETS ON NAMES.

I.

EDITH.

A LILY with its frail cup filled with dew,
Down-bending modestly, snow-white and pale,
Shedding faint fragrance round its native vale,
Minds me of thee, sweet Edith, mild and true,
And of thy eyes so innocent and blue,
Thy heart is fearful as a startled hare,
Yet hath in it a fortitude to bear
For Love's sake, and a gentle faith which grew
Of Love : need of a stay whereon to lean,
Felt in thyself, hath taught thee to uphold
And comfort others, and to give, unseen,
The kindness thy still love cannot withhold :
Maiden, I would my sister thou hadst been,
That round thee I my guarding arms might
  fold.

II.

ROSE.

MY ever-lightsome, ever-laughing Rose,
Who always speakest first and thinkest last,
Thy full voice is as clear as bugle-blast;
Right from the ear down to the heart it goes
And says, " I'm beautiful! as who but knows?"

Thy name reminds me of old romping days,
Of kisses stolen in dark passage-ways,
Or in the parlor, if the mother-nose
Gave sign of drowsy watch. I wonder where
Are gone thy tokens, given with a glance
So full of everlasting love till morrow,
Or a day's endless grieving for the dance
Last night denied, backed with a lock of hair,
That spake of broken hearts and deadly sorrow.

III.

MARY.

DARK hair, dark eyes—not too dark to be deep
And full of feeling, yet enough to glow
With fire when angered; feelings never slow,
But which seem rather watching to forthleap
From her full breast; a gently-flowing sweep
Of words in common talk, a torrent-rush,
Whenever through her soul swift feelings gush,
A heart less ready to be gay than weep,
Yet cheerful ever; a calm matron-smile,
That bids God bless you; a chaste simpleness,
With somewhat, too, of "proper pride," in
        dress;—
This portrait to my mind's eye came, the while
I thought of thee, the well-grown woman Mary,
Whilome a gold-haired laughing little fairy.

IV.

CAROLINE.

A STAIDNESS sobers o'er her pretty face,
Which something but ill-hidden in her eyes,

And a quaint look about her lips denies;
A lingering love of girlhood you can trace
In her checked laugh and half-restrainèd pace;
And, when she bears herself most womanly,
It seems as if a watchful mother's eye
Kept down with sobering glance her childish
    grace:
Yet oftentimes her nature gushes free
As water long held back by little hands,
Within a pump, and let forth suddenly,
Until, her task remembering, she stands
A moment silent, smiling doubtfully,
Then laughs aloud and scorns her hated bands.

v.

ANNE.

THERE is a pensiveness in quiet Anne,
A mournful drooping of the full gray eye,
As if she had shook hands with misery,
And known some care since her short life began;
Her cheek is seriously pale, nigh wan,
And, though of cheerfulness there is no lack,
You feel as if she must be dressed in black;
Yet is she not of those who, all they can,
Strive to be gay, and striving, seem most sad—
Hers is not grief, but silent soberness;
You would be startled if you saw her glad,
And startled if you saw her weep, no less;
She walks through life, as, on the Sabbath
    day,
She decorously glides to church to pray.

www.ingramcontent.com/pod-product-compliance
Lightning Source LLC
Chambersburg PA
CBHW030637150426
42813CB00050B/72